MONEY

A MARKET-ORIENTED APPROACH

WILLIAM D. GERDES

PROFESSOR OF ECONOMICS, CLARKE COLLEGE

GROOTHUSEN PRESS
DUBUQUE, IOWA
2006

Groothusen Press

2255 Yorktown Road

Dubuque, IA 52002

Library of Congress Control Number: 2006906558

ISBN: 0-9787578-0-7

ISBN: 978-0-9787578-0-9

Printed in the United States by Morris Publishing
3212 East Highway 30
Kearney, NE 68847
1-800-650-7888

TABLE OF CONTENTS

Chapter 1   Money and Monetary Systems 1

Chapter 2   Interest Rates and Financial Markets 28

Chapter 3   Money and Foreign Exchange Markets...................79

Chapter 4   Central Banks and the Money Supply...................149

Chapter 5   Money and Income...192

Chapter 6   Monetary Policy 208

Chapter 7   Critiques of Monetary Policy....................................238

CHAPTER 1

MONEY AND MONETARY SYSTEMS

I.   Money, Barter, and Exchange 2

II. The Origins of Money 5

III. Secondary Functions of Money 6

IV. Types of Monetary Systems 8

      A. Commodity Money 9

      B. Fiduciary Money 11

      C. Fiat Money 17

V.   Properties of Money 20

VI. Measures of Money 22

VII. Inflation, Deflation, and the Value of Money 24

I. Money, Barter, and Exchange

Aside from the act of production, voluntary exchange is the major means available for individuals to improve their material well being. When two individuals engage in an exchange, the motive of each is to improve his or her welfare. The result, however, is their mutual betterment since both parties gain as a consequence of the transaction. The potential for exchange also contributes to material living standards in another important way. It allows for greater specialization in production, which generally increases the level of output.

There are two forms of voluntary exchange: 1) barter; and, 2) those involving money. Barter is the direct exchange, where goods and services are exchanged for other goods and services (G $\longleftrightarrow$ G). A requisite for a barter transaction is the existence of a double coincidence of wants. Individual A, for example, possesses wheat but would like to exchange some of that wheat for a baseball glove. That individual must find another (individual B) who has a baseball glove he is willing to exchange for some wheat. If there are two such individuals, a double coincidence of wants is said to exist. If they find one another, and mutually agree on a rate of exchange, an exchange occurs.

Exchange involving the use of money is called indirect exchange. Rather than a direct exchange of goods as in barter, goods are exchanged for an intermediate good (money) which is then exchanged for other goods and services (G $\rightarrow$ M $\rightarrow$ G). At first, this appears to be less efficient since it requires an extra transaction. If it were less efficient, however, individuals would prefer barter to the use of money. In practice, it works out quite differently. Nearly all transactions involve the use of money.

What is money, and why is it that monetary transactions are the dominant form of exchange? Money is any generally accepted medium of exchange. It is not a product of government, since its use predates modern forms of government. Likewise, it is not something bestowed upon us by deities. Rather, it is a behavioral phenomenon. It is whatever individuals opt to use as an exchange medium.

The concept of money is necessarily dynamic because what people use as an exchange medium varies with time and place. In virtually every culture, money in use today differs from that of the past. Moreover, at any point in time, one can observe different forms of money used in different locations. Money used for purchases in an African village market is different from money used to settle bond transactions in the world's major money centers. Both are different from that used in an isolated subculture in Papa New Guinea.

Economists generally introduce the concept of transactions costs to explain the dominance of monetary over barter transactions. Transactions costs are the resources that individuals must invest in order to participate in exchanges. An example is the time and effort required to carry a bag of wheat to the market. The nearly universal preference for the use of money in exchanges indicates that transactions-costs generally are lower in money transactions than in barter transactions.

There are three principal types of transactions costs: 1) information costs; 2) transportation costs; and, 3) storage costs. Information is not a free good. If it were, quantities and offer prices for all goods and services would be known by everyone. Since a single individual does not possess all this information, resources frequently must be invested to acquire additional information prior to an exchange. In the barter example above, the individual with wheat must use resources to seek out an individual with a baseball glove. Once a generally accepted exchange medium is in use, it generally requires fewer resources to sell the wheat for money, and to use the money to purchase a baseball glove. With fewer resources expended, the transactions costs of exchange are reduced.

A second type of transactions cost is transportation costs. Parties to an exchange must transport those items to be exchanged. Most monies are relatively easy to transport, and one can do so at a relatively low cost. It is not very difficult, for example, to carry one's wallet or checkbook to the market. In a barter economy, individuals often must transport commodities (such as wheat) to the market at considerably higher cost. Thus, use of money normally reduces transactions costs due to the relative ease of transporting it to the market.

Finally, storage costs arise because of the necessity of storing items that are to be traded. Like other transactions costs, they normally can not be avoided. The best one can hope to do is to limit them. Storage costs in barter tend to be relatively high because of the greater number of commodities one must inventory, and because some of them deteriorate while in storage. An example of the latter is grain spoilage that occurs during the holding period. By contrast, money is much simpler to store although there are storage costs here, too. Today, they often assume the form of either service fees charged to holders of bank accounts or the erosion in the purchasing power of money due to inflation. Storage costs due to higher inflation rates have become a much more significant monetary phenomenon following the imposition of fiat money, a form of money discussed below.

II. The Origins of Money

Transactions costs are not only useful in explaining the dominance of money over barter, but they also help in explaining the origins of money. While we do not know where or when money was first used, Austrian economist Carl Menger provided an insightful hypothesis about how this most likely occurred.[1] Money, he argued, was a spontaneous market development. It was not something invented by a prescient government, or brought to us via the auspices of well-meaning religious leaders. No one individual or group of individuals can take credit for its development.

Instead, money evolved in the marketplace as self-interested individuals strived to reduce their transactions costs in effectuating exchanges. In doing so, they often "traded up" in terms of liquidity, or what Menger referred to as saleability. That is, individuals accepted in exchange an item that they did not desire for their own use but, rather, something that was more liquid than what they had to offer in exchange. Through ownership of a more liquid good, they hoped to acquire their desired good (or goods) more easily, i.e., with lower transactions costs.

In the process of making exchanges, it is quite likely that individuals had similar perceptions concerning which goods possessed greater liquidity. The origin of money took place once individuals commenced using, with regularity, the same intermediate good for this purpose. That good became the first money.

---

[1] See Carl Menger, "On the Origins of Money," *Economic Journal*, 2, June, 1892, 239-255.

III. Secondary Functions of Money

While money is defined in terms of its primary function (medium of exchange), it serves other functions as well: as a store of value, unit of account, and standard of deferred payment. Its usefulness in these other functions, however, most often is the direct result of its use as a medium of exchange. That is why they are referred to as secondary functions.

Money is a vehicle for transferring purchasing power through time. In this sense, it serves as a store of value. It performs this function even when it is held for relatively short periods as an exchange medium. But, it can do so as well when it is held for longer periods as a form of accumulated wealth.

Money is not unique in performing this function. Individuals hold various types of non-monetary financial assets such as time and saving deposits at banks, government and corporate bonds, and equities (or ownership in private corporations). In addition, wealth is accumulated in the form of real assets. Examples are land, buildings, jewelry, and paintings. Despite these alternative forms of holding wealth, nearly all individuals hold a portion of their wealth in the form of money. A major reason for doing so is that money is the most liquid of assets. That is, it gives its holder immediate access to markets.

Money also serves as a unit of account (or measure of value). In a monetary economy, the exchange value of all goods and services are quoted in terms of money, and comparative valuations are made by referring to monetary values of objects. Entries in financial statements (such as balance sheets and income statements) also are recorded in money terms. There are good reasons for using money in this way. If it were not the case, it would be much more difficult to make relative comparisons. Individuals making exchanges would necessarily make many additional conversions, and transactions costs would increase commensurately.

To illustrate money's importance as a unit of account, consider an economy with ten goods. One of them is money. Using money as a unit of account, a complete knowledge of prices in this economy would include the prices of the nine non-monetary goods. In contrast, if this were a ten-good barter economy, one potentially must know the exchange value (or price) of each good relative to each of the other nine goods. There are 90 such exchange ratios, or 45 if one treats exchange ratios that are reciprocals as the same price. Moreover, the discrepancy in the potential number of prices one must know increases geometrically as the number of goods in the economy increases.[2] It follows that the use of money, as opposed to barter, significantly reduces the information costs (or number of prices) necessary for engaging in market exchange.

A final function of money is that it is customary to write loan contacts in terms of money. In this function, money is referred to as a standard of deferred payment. It is not necessary that money serve this function. It is possible, for example, to write a loan contract in which the proceeds of the loan (and subsequent repayment) are payable in corn, wheat, or any other commodity. It is unlikely, however, that both parties to a loan contract would find one of these commodities agreeable. As a consequence, virtually all

---

[2] The number of elements in a matrix of exchange rates for an n-good economy is n^2. All the elements on the main diagonal have a value of one, since the rate of exchange of a good for itself is 1:1. Hence, the number of non-trivial exchange ratios is $n^2 - n$, or $n(n-1)$. For off-diagonal elements, the value of a_{ij} is the reciprocal of a_{ji}. They both represent the price for the same pair of goods expressed in two different ways: the number of units of good i which exchanges for one unit of good j, and the number of units of good j which exchanges for one unit of good i. By treating each of these pairs as a single price, the number of non-trivial and unique prices (N) in an n-good barter economy is halved: $N = n(n-1)/2$. For $n = 10$, $N = 45$. Notice that as the number of goods in a barter economy grows, the number of prices an economic agent potentially must know increases geometrically.

credit contracts involve payment in money, and it is reasonable to presume that doing so significantly increases the volume of activity in credit markets.

Despite its widespread usage, there are times when money does not serve well as a standard of deferred payment. This normally occurs when changes in the purchasing power of money are very unpredictable. During these periods, writing credit contracts in money terms results in considerable risk exposure for borrowers and lenders. They often prefer to have loans repaid in real purchasing power, with actual repayment determined at the end of the contract period. A common way to do this is to tie the value of money repayment to a price index, or some measure of movement in the general price level. In this case, commodities rather than money are used as the standard of deferred payment. This practice is known as indexing.

IV. Types of Monetary Systems

There are three general types of monetary systems: commodity, fiduciary, and fiat.[3] Nearly all of our accumulated monetary experience is with commodity money. Fiduciary elements were introduced only in recent centuries, and it was not until the twentieth century that nearly every society converted to the use of fiat money. From a broad historical perspective, then, the type of money used by nearly everyone today is a relatively new phenomenon.

---

[3] For an extended version of this discussion of monetary systems, see William D. Gerdes, "A Taxonomy of Monies from the Consumer's Perspective," *The Journal of Economics,* (28) 2, 1997.

A. Commodity Money

Commodity money is money whose value (at the margin) when used for monetary purposes tends toward equivalency with its value (at the margin) when used for non-monetary purposes. This form of money emerged spontaneously in the marketplace, as individuals attempted to reduce their transactions costs in effectuating exchanges. Although a great number of different objects have been used as commodity money, precious metals were the most popular. Bronze, iron, and, more recently, silver and gold are metals that have been most widely used for this purpose.

The theory of consumer behavior can be utilized in examining the nature of commodity money. Consider a consuming unit that is acting in its own self-interest. Three goods are available for consumption: a single commodity (C), monetary gold (GM), and gold used for a single non-monetary purpose such as jewelry (GNM). The consuming unit has a fixed amount of wealth (W) that it will allocate among these three goods. Such a situation normally is modeled as a constrained maximization problem, where an economic agent maximizes its utility function subject to its wealth constraint. The wealth constraint is written as an equality because the consuming unit is assumed to spend all of its wealth.

1.1) Max $U = f(C, G_M, G_{NM})$ subject to

$$W = P_C C + P_{GM} G_M + P_{GNM} G_{NM},$$

where U is total utility or total satisfaction, and
P_C, P_{GM}, and P_{GNM} are the prices of C, GM, and GNM respectively.

When the consuming unit does maximize its utility function (or acts in its own self-interest), the following string of equalities holds.

$$1.2) \quad MU_c / P_c = MU_{GM} / P_{GM} = MU_{GNM} / P_{GNM}$$

The ratio of the marginal utility (MU) to the price for each of the three goods is the same. The last equality in equation 1.2), i.e., $MU_{GM} / P_{GM} = MU_{GNM} / P_{GNM}$, is simply a more formal statement of the definition of commodity money. It makes no difference to the consumer whether the last unit of money is used to purchase money balances or used to purchase non-monetary gold. Both yield the same amount of satisfaction. Money has equivalent subjective value in monetary and nonmonetary uses.

It is the maximizing behavior by economic agents that assures us of this outcome. If equality 1.2) does not hold, an individual can obtain a greater amount of total utility with no increase in its wealth. Assume, for example, that inequality 1.3) holds.

$$1.3) \quad MU_{GM} / P_{GM} < MU_{GNM} / P_{GNM}$$

For this economic agent, the last unit of money held as monetary gold (GM) yields less satisfaction than the last unit of money used to purchase non-monetary gold (GNM). With no increase in its resources (wealth), this economic agent can exchange monetary gold for non-monetary gold and increase its well being. This increase occurs in the form of a rise in total utility, or total satisfaction. Self-interest will spur the economic agent to continue this substitution until it is no longer beneficial. That occurs only when the two ratios are again equal to one another as in equation 1.2).

If inequality 1.3) holds for many individuals simultaneously, the money supply in the economy will fall as economic agents melt down monetary gold and use it for non-monetary purposes. Likewise, a greater than inequality will cause the money supply to increase. Individual economic agents determine the optimal use of the commodity employed as commodity money. Their actions, collectively, determine the size of the money stock.

B. Fiduciary Money

Fiduciary money differs from commodity money in two respects. First, its value (at the margin) when used for monetary purposes exceeds its value (at the margin) when used for non-monetary purposes. For that reason, one does not observe individuals using fiduciary money for non-monetary purposes.

Fiduciary money differs from commodity money in another important respect. It has a convertibility option. It is a (paper) contract to pay a specified amount of commodity money on demand. For example, printed on a ten-dollar bill is the statement "Pay to the Bearer on Demand: Ten Dollars." When this note is presented to the issuer, the issuer is obliged to pay the bearer ten dollars in monetary gold.

In the evolution of money as an exchange medium, business enterprises commenced to provide the service of safekeeping commodity money for those who did not wish to keep their accumulated money holdings in their homes. Individuals would bring monetary gold to the business for storage and receive a (paper) receipt acknowledging the deposit. Businesses would charge a small fee for this service, or might possibility do it without charge for a friend or regular business customer. Most likely it was goldsmiths who provided this service because it was necessary for them to secure inventories of gold as a normal part of their business activity. It also is quite probable that banking originated in this manner, since these goldsmiths were performing what is called the depository function of banks. Thus, it is common to refer to goldsmiths performing this function as early bankers.

When an individual wanted to make a purchase, he/she would go to the goldsmith, withdraw money, and exchange it for the item of interest. In a village or small town, it is quite possible that the individual receiving the gold coins would take them to the same goldsmith for deposit. Transactions costs were lower if the first individual simply transferred ownership of the deposit (by offering the warehouse receipt issued by the goldsmith) to the second individual. Doing so saved both a trip to the goldsmith. Once this started to happen, what people were using as an exchange medium had changed. They now were making purchases with commodity money and with paper claims on this money. The paper claims were serving as fiduciary money.

The money supply is unaffected by the use of fiduciary money so long as goldsmiths/bankers practice 100% reserve banking, and gold coins deposited with goldsmiths are excluded from the measure of the money. Banking institutions practice 100% reserve banking if they always hold monetary reserves in the proportion of 100% of their deposit liabilities. This is the case for the goldsmith whose balance sheet appears in EXHIBIT 1.1(A). Reserves of monetary gold held as an asset are equal to 100. So, too, are receipts issued by the firm (that are payable in commodity money on demand). They are liabilities of the goldsmith/banker.

Banks practicing 100% reserve banking are simply warehousing money. They do not create it. To illustrate, measure the money supply as the total amount of commodity

---

EXHIBIT 1.1

Balance Sheet of Goldsmith / Banker

(A)

Assets		Liabilities	
Gold Coins	100	Receipts Issued	100

(B)

Assets		Liabilities	
Gold Coins	80	Receipts Issued	100
Loans	20		

(C)

Assets		Liabilities	
Gold Coins	100	Receipts Issued	120
Loans	20		

money circulating outside banks (G_M) plus the total amount of bank-issued fiduciary money (FG_M, or fiduciary money used for monetary purposes). This measure appears in equation 1.4). So long as banks practice 100% reserve banking, whenever someone makes a deposit, circulating commodity money falls by exactly the same amount as fiduciary money increases (equation 1.5). Withdrawals, likewise, do not affect the money supply. Individuals simply exchange fiduciary money for commodity money on a one-for-one basis with banks.

$$1.4) \quad M = G_M + FG_M$$

$$1.5) \quad M \rightarrow = G_M \downarrow + FG_M \uparrow$$

Banks do, however, affect the money supply when they practice fractional reserve banking. In this case, banks hold monetary reserves in some fraction (less than 1) of their deposit liabilities. Assume that our goldsmith observes two things. First, gold coins are anonymous. If you withdraw gold and the goldsmith gives you coins that someone else deposited, you will not know the difference. Moreover, you will not care so long as you receive coins of equivalent value. Second, on any given day some individuals deposit gold coins. Others withdraw them. It never occurs that all individuals wish to withdraw on the same day, and that there are no depositors that day. Hence, from the perspective of the goldsmith, it is unnecessary to hold 100% reserves to cover deposit liabilities payable on demand.

These two phenomena allow the goldsmith to extend its banking functions by making loans. If a customer wishes to borrow, the banker feels comfortable in making the loan. The incentive for doing so is the higher profits that result from interest payments on the loan. By making the loan, the goldsmith has moved from 100% reserve banking to fractional reserve banking. This has enormous monetary consequences because banks practicing fractional reserve banking are no longer simply storing money. They are also affecting the size of the money supply. This occurs because the proceeds of the bank loan become a net addition to the money stock.

The effect on the money supply is the same whether the proceeds of the loan are made available in the form of commodity money or fiduciary money. Balance sheets (B) and (C) in EXHIBIT 1.1 show the impacts on the goldsmith's balance sheet. In balance sheet (B), the proceeds of the loan are in the form of commodity money. Note that the goldsmith's holdings of gold coins are down by 20, but that he now has a promissory note (signed by the borrower) valued at 20. The 20 in gold coins that are no longer owned by the banker are now a part of circulating commodity money. Since the quantity of fiduciary money is the same as it was before, the money supply has increased by 20 (the amount of the loan).

In balance sheet (C), the proceeds of the loan are made available in the form of fiduciary money. In this case, the goldsmith owns a promissory note that he acquired by issuing the fiduciary money. Since the quantity of circulating commodity money now is the same as it was before, the money supply has increased by 20 (the amount of the loan). Balance sheets (B) and (C) reveal that our goldsmith is now practicing fractional reserve banking. Reserves of gold coins are less than the amount of fiduciary money issued.

If we extend the analysis of consumer behavior to include fiduciary money, the consuming unit now has additional choices. When allocating its wealth, it now can choose quantities of the single commodity (C), monetary gold (G_M), non-monetary gold (G_{NM}), fiduciary money held for monetary purposes (FG_M), and fiduciary money held for non-monetary purposes (FG_{NM}). The consumer again maximizes a constrained utility function, as shown in 1.6).

1.6) Max. $U = f(C, G_M, G_{NM}, FG_M, FG_{NM})$

subject to $W = P_c C + P_{GM} G_M + P_{GNM} G_{NM} + P_{FGM} FG_M + P_{FGNM} FG_{NM}$

Because fiduciary money is made of paper, there are a variety of potential nonmonetary uses of that money. For example, one could use it to wallpaper the bedroom, to light one's cigar, or as napkins at the evening meal. In practice, one does not see fiduciary money used for these purposes. That is, the quantity of fiduciary money used for non-monetary purposes tends to be zero. When this is the case, and our consuming unit is maximizing the above utility function, the following condition holds.

1.7) $MU_C/P_C = MU_{GM}/P_{GM} = MU_{GNM}/P_{GNM} = MU_{FGM}/P_{FGM} > MU_{FGNM}/P_{FGNM}$

The ratio of the marginal utility to the price is the same for each good with the exception of the last inequality. This inequality is a more formal way of stating the first major feature of fiduciary money. The value of fiduciary money (at the margin) when used for monetary purposes exceeds its value (at the margin) when used for non-monetary purposes.[4]

---

[4] The inequality occurs because of (non-negativity) constraints on the consuming unit. The consumer(s) can not hold a negative quantity of any commodity. Once no fiduciary money is used for non-monetary

Although people often identify it as a commodity money system, the gold standard of the nineteenth and early twentieth centuries is a prime example of fiduciary money. The confusion exists because all fiduciary monetary systems are "hybrid" arrangements. In this case, commodity money in the form of gold coins was used as an exchange medium along with fiduciary money which was convertible into commodity money on demand.

C. Fiat Money

Governments replaced fiduciary money arrangements with the fiat money standard currently in use. Fiat money has two distinctive features. Like fiduciary money, it has the property that its value (at the margin) when used as money exceeds its value (at the margin) when used for non-monetary purposes.[5] The difference is the convertibility option. Fiduciary money is convertible (at issuing institutions) into commodity money on demand; fiat money is not.

This distinction is critical in understanding the origins of fiat money. Unlike commodity and fiduciary monies, fiat money was not a spontaneous market development. It did not result from the spontaneous efforts of market participants to lower their transactions costs. Instead, it came about through the efforts of governments to gain control over money. By now quite active in the monetary process, governments invoked laws abrogating the convertibility option. Although this most recently happened in the 1930s, the history of fiduciary money standards is marked by episodes where

---

purposes, further substitution of FG_M for FG_{NM} is not possible---even if the marginal value of the last unit of wealth spent on FG_M exceeds the marginal value of the last unit spent on FG_{NM}.

[5] It is erroneous to assert, as some economists do, that fiat money has no intrinsic value. From this perspective, the marginal subjective value of fiat money, when used for nonmonetary purposes, is zero. We know that is not the case. The examples of nonmonetary uses for fiduciary money (cited above) are also possible uses of fiat money. Additional potential uses for stacks of fiat money are as doorstops, paperweights, or as kindling in the fireplace.

governments suspended the convertibility option that is the centerpiece of any fiduciary money system.

Governments found it especially difficult to refrain from doing this during wartime. They were anxious to gain claims on more resources in order to prosecute the war effort. Although higher taxes always were an option, governments most often opted instead for printing more money. This choice places considerable stress on a fiduciary money system by significantly increasing the quantity of fiduciary money in use relative to commodity money. Ultimately, this jeopardizes the ability of issuers of fiduciary money to convert that money back into commodity money on demand. As a way around this problem, governments often passed laws suspending convertibility. Great Britain did this during the Napoleonic Wars as did the major adversaries during World War I.

The politics (and economics) of reestablishing fiduciary money arrangements after wars ended were both tedious and divisive. It took Great Britain nearly a decade to restore the gold standard after World War I. Shortly after she had done so, the major trading countries were caught in the midst of the Great Depression. Once again they suspended convertibility, but this time it was not viewed as a temporary expedient. Governments were eager to wrest control of money from the private sector.

By now, however, individuals were quite accustomed to using paper money to effectuate exchanges. Under the fiduciary money standard, most individuals opted to make payment with paper money because of lower transactions costs. Thus, movement to the fiat money standard did not require a significant modification of their behavior. Nonetheless, consumers did have a preference for fiduciary money.[6] That meant that

---

[6] Had consumers preferred fiat money, issuers of fiduciary money would have voluntarily accommodated those preferences.

governments (such as that in the United States) found it necessary to impose laws making it illegal for individuals to hold commodity money in order to discourage further usage.

From the theory of consumer choice, the analysis of fiat money is not greatly different from that of fiduciary money. Assuming government confiscation of all monetary gold, variables in the individual utility function are the same as equation 1.6) with two exceptions. Monetary gold (G_M) does not appear, and fiduciary money (FG) is replaced by fiat money (FM). When the consuming unit maximizes utility subject to a wealth constraint, the relation 1.8) holds.

$$1.8) \quad MU_c/P_c = MU_{GNM}/P_{GNM} = MU_{FMM}/P_{FMM} > MU_{FMN}/P_{FMN}$$

Two things are worthy of note here. First, the relation is similar to 1.7). The differences are that monetary gold no longer appears, and fiat money replaces fiduciary money. Second, like fiduciary money, fiat money tends not to be used for non-monetary purposes. If none is used for this purpose, and the value (at the margin) of fiat money used for monetary purposes exceeds its value (at the margin) when used non-monetary purposes, the last inequality in relation 1.8) obtains.

EXHIBIT 1.2 summarizes the differences among the three monetary arrangements. The differentiating characteristics are: 1) whether money has the same value when used for monetary and non-monetary purposes; and, 2) whether money is convertible into a specified amount of commodity money on demand (at financial institutions).

EXHIBIT 1.2

Characteristics of Different Monies

Type of Money	Equivalent Value in Monetary and Nonmonetary Use	Greater Value in In Monetary Use	Convertibility Option
Commodity	X		
Fiduciary		X	X
Fiat		X	

V.   Properties of Money

Many different objects have served as money. This is especially true for commodity money, where cattle, sea-shells, beads, calico cloth, animal skins, tobacco, and precious metals all were used at one time or another. Despite the great variety of objects that have served as money, there are certain properties that all monies tend to possess. Each form of money, of course, possesses them in a different degree. Because these properties relate to the transactions costs of using money in exchange, they add credence to Menger's proposition that reducing transactions cost is crucial in the selection of a particular object for use as money.

Four properties of money are discussed here. The first is portability. Most objects selected for use as money can be readily transported to the market. Animal skins are more portable than are animals; metals coins more portable than animal skins; and, paper money more portable than metal coins. It is apparent that reducing transactions costs through greater portability was an important consideration in the evolution of money.

A second common property of money is divisibility. In the marketplace, items with a wide range of exchange values are traded. Money that is more divisible has greater value because it can be used in purchasing both relatively high and relatively low value goods. Cattle, when used as money, do not have this divisibility feature. Precious metals do, as do the more modern forms of money.

Third, most monies are durable. If money does not have this property, it will lose exchange value between the time it is accepted in exchange and the time when it is offered again in exchange. This probably explains why precious metals were a preferred form of commodity money. Even with the adoption of paper money, durability remains a matter of concern. Issuing governments want to know how soon such money will have to be replaced as a consequence of wear and tear.

Finally, most monies are objects that are relatively scarce. Transactions costs tend to be high when an object is used that is not scarce. That is because there is a high probability that such money will lose exchange value during the holding period. Precious metals, once again, are an example of money that is not easily augmentable. The production costs of doing so generally are substantial. Paper money, on the other hand, can be readily augmented in a short period of time. Our experiment with fiat money in the past century reveals that this is one of the problems associated with using such money.

VI. Measures of Money

There are several different measures money. Two are discussed here: M1 and M2. The M1 measure, which is sometimes called the "narrow" measure, most closely conforms to the definition of money as a generally accepted exchange medium. Depicted in 1.9), it consists of currency in circulation outside banks (C), demand deposits other than those owned by the central government (DD), and other checkable deposits (OCD). When demand deposits and other checkable deposits are aggregated, they are designated as DD√.

$$1.9) \quad M1 = C + DD + OCD$$
$$= C + DD√$$

Currency is the total of all circulating coins and paper notes. In the past, they frequently were issued by private businesses, but they now are largely in the domain of governments. In the U.S., the Treasury issues all coins, while the Federal Reserve System issues paper notes. Demand deposits are checking balances at depository institutions that are payable on demand. Such deposits are widely used in making exchanges.

Since the great depression, U.S. banks have not been permitted to pay interest on these deposits. In the post-World War II period, this placed banking institutions at a competitive disadvantage in the financial marketplace. They responded (in the 1970s) by issuing savings deposits that allowed individuals to access funds in these accounts by writing a check. Examples are share drafts and NOW (negotiable order of withdrawal) accounts. These interest-bearing checking accounts became popular and, beginning in 1980, they were included in the M1 measure as other checkable deposits (OCD). They are so classified because, from a legal standpoint, they are not demand deposits.

A second measure of money is M2. It consists of all of the instruments in M1 plus additional financial instruments that have check-writing privileges (certain money market deposit accounts and money market mutual funds shares). It also includes other financial instruments that are closely substitutable for checking deposits. These instruments typically are very liquid and can be converted into deposit money with very low transactions costs. Included on these grounds are small-denomination time deposits, saving deposits (without check-writing privileges), overnight repurchase agreements, and certain overnight Eurodollar balances.

While M1 more closely conforms to the definition of money, for a number of reasons the M2 measure is often preferred. A major one is that the quality of the M1 measure has deteriorated since 1994, when banks commenced reclassifying a portion of their M1 liabilities into liabilities that are not included in M1. The motive was to reduce a bank's required reserves. This issue is discussed in more detail in Chapter 4.

VII.   Inflation, Deflation, and the Value of Money

The exchange value of money is the amount of purchasing power that money possesses. While one of the functions of money is the unit of account function, it is not fruitful to express the exchange value of money in terms of money. Doing so always yields the trivial value of one. The number of U.S. dollars that exchanges for one unit of money (one dollar), for example, is precisely one. Likewise, the number of British pounds that exchanges for one unit of money (one pound) is also one.

With money viewed as generalized purchasing power, its exchange value is considered, instead, in terms of how money exchanges against all other things. In this sense, the exchange value of money, or the purchasing power of money (PPM), is the reciprocal of the average price (P).

1.10) $PPM = 1/P$

The average price is sometimes called the price level. It is the weighted average of individual prices of things other than money. In equation 1.11), these other things are represented by prices $P_1, P_2, \ldots\ldots P_n$. Note that an increase in P (and a decrease in PPM) does not imply that all other prices increase. It simply means that the average of these prices is now higher.

1.11) $P = \overline{(P_1, P_2, \ldots\ldots, P_n)}$

The exchange value of money is subject to continuous variation. Money loses value relative to goods and services when the general price level is increasing. It now takes more units of money to purchase goods and services in general. Situations when P is increasing (and the PPM is decreasing) are known as inflation. Deflation occurs when the exchange value of money is increasing. Fewer units of money generally are required to purchase a given quantity of goods and services. P is declining and the PPM is increasing.

How much the exchange value of money changes depends on the type of monetary system in use. That has certainly been true in the United States. Figure 1.1 shows the price level for the U.S. economy from the Revolutionary War period to early in the twenty-first century. In 1933, the average price was approximately 6 percent lower than it was in 1780. There were episodes of inflation and deflation between these dates but, on a secular basis, the country experienced general price stability. With few exceptions, this period was characterized by the use of commodity and fiduciary monies.

Through an executive order, President Roosevelt moved the U.S. off the gold standard (fiduciary money) in March of 1933, and country was now on a fiat money standard. In Figure 1.1, it is easy to see when the change in monetary regimes occurred. With fiduciary money, the convertibility option constrained how much money the government could print. That constraint does not exist with fiat money. The result has been secular inflation.

The exodus from fiduciary money in the 1930s was international in scope. The principal motive was to give government greater control over money. That objective was achieved. What governments accomplished with their enhanced monetary powers has

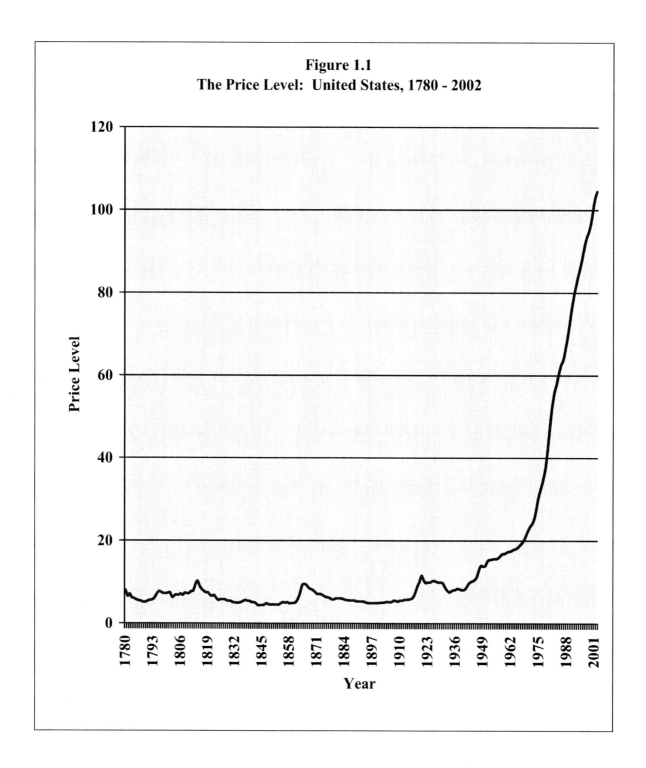

Figure 1.1
The Price Level: United States, 1780 - 2002

Sources: McCusker, Johon J., *How Much is that in Real Money?*, American Antiquarian
Society, 2001. Consumer Price Index , U.S. Bureau of Labor Statistics,
1974-2002.

generally been unimpressive. This is especially true with respect to maintaining money's integrity. Since the introduction of fiat money, the exchange value of money has, with few exceptions, continuously declined. In the U.S., the dollar lost approximately 93 percent of its purchasing power from 1933 to 2002. The performance was much worse in most other countries. For observations on how poorly governments, in general, have performed, see TABLE 6.2 (page 214).

CHAPTER 2

INTEREST RATES AND FINANCIAL MARKETS

I.   **Financial Markets** 29

    A. Classification of Participants in Financial Markets...........29
        i) **Savings-Surplus Units** 32
        ii) **Savings-Deficit Units** 33

    B. Financial Flows...34

II.   **Intertemporal Production and Exchange** 38

    A. Marginal Productivity of Capital 38

    B. Price of Credit..39

    C. Marginal Rate of Time Preference 40

    D. Defining Interest...42

III. **Interest Rates** 43

    A. The Real Interest Rate...43
        i) **The Positive Real Rate of Interest** 44
        ii) **The Level of the Real Interest Rate** 46
        iii) **Risk and the Real Rate of Interest**......................49

    B. The Nominal Interest Rate 52
        i) **Bond Prices and Interest Rates** 53
        ii) **Inflationary Expectations** 55
        iii) **The Vector of Nominal Interest Rates**...................63

IV. **The Term Structure of Interest Rates**...............................65

    A. Forward Rates...66

    B. Unbiased Expectations Theory 69

    C. Liquidity Preference Theory......................................73

    D. Market Segmentation Theory 76

I. Financial Markets

Financial instruments are traded in financial markets. The instruments are of two types. Equity instruments represent ownership in businesses, and are most often traded on organized stock exchanges. Debt instruments, or bonds, represent the borrowing of one economic agent from another. Organized exchanges where these instruments are traded are called bond markets.

Financial markets are critical for economic growth. The reason is that financial markets facilitate capital formation. Capital formation is important because the use of capital goods generally enhances human productivity. Hence, the availability and widespread use of capital goods is one of the prominent characteristics of relatively affluent countries. Relatively poor countries are characterized by the opposite----the limited use of capital goods and heavy reliance on human labor to carry out production. It is not surprising, then, that countries that discourage the development of financial markets generally languish. Those countries that encourage their development most often prosper.

A. Classification of Participants in Financial Markets

Saving, or the abstinence from consumption, is a requisite for capital formation. The act of saving releases resources for the production of capital goods, or real investment. The production possibilities curve in FIGURE 2.1 shows this trade-off between consumption and investment. Each point on the curve is an ordered pair that represents an output combination that it is possible to produce. Constraints in effect include a given stock of resources and a given state of technology.

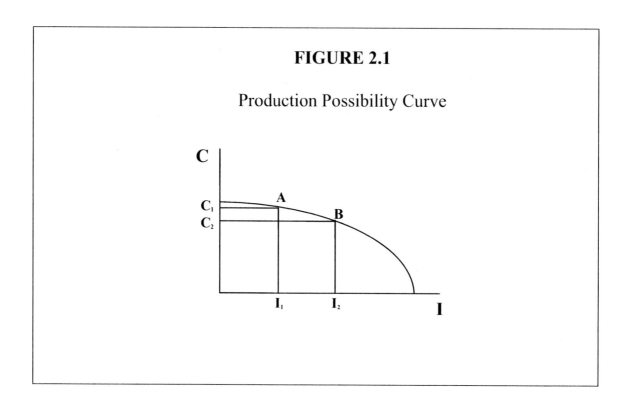

FIGURE 2.1

Production Possibility Curve

Movement along the curve from point A to point B, for example, requires additional saving. More saving results in increased investment, and the production of capital goods increases from I_1 to I_2. This additional capital formation is made possible by abstinence from consumption, which falls from C_1 to C_2.

Flow of funds accounts, which provide a record of a country's financial flows, include an accounting identity that relates saving and investment. In the aggregate, total saving (S) is precisely equal to total investment (I).

2.1) $S \equiv I$

Saving and capital formation can take place in an economy without financial markets. However, all capital formation must be internally financed. That is, the economic unit purchasing the capital goods must also provide the saving to finance that purchase.[7] In such an economy, aggregate identity 2.1) also holds for each individual economic unit.

The introduction of financial markets greatly increases the potential for capital formation. Now it is possible for the saving of one individual economic unit to finance the capital goods purchase of another economic unit. Because those wishing to purchase a capital good are no longer required to provide the requisite saving, the potential for capital formation is greatly enhanced. By facilitating capital formation, financial markets contribute in a significant way to the economic welfare of a society.

In an economy with financial markets, identity 2.1) still holds in the aggregate. However, it no longer must hold for individual economic units. Moreover, the relationship between saving and investment for the individual economic unit now serves as the criterion for classifying participation in financial markets. Economic units whose saving exceeds their investment are called savings-surplus units. Those with investment greater than their saving are classified as savings-deficit units. Knife's-edge cases where saving is exactly equal to investment are neither savings-surplus nor savings-deficit units.[8]

---

[7] An economic unit is a decision-making entity. These units are generally classified as a household, business, or governmental unit.

[8] This method for classifying participation was employed by James C. Van Horne, *Financial Market Rates and Flows* (Englewood Cliffs, NJ: Prentice-Hall, 5th ed., 1998). It was also used in early flow-of-funds studies. See Goldsmith, Raymond, *The Flow of Capital funds in the Postwar Economy* (New York: National Bureau of Economic Research, 1965).

i) Savings-Surplus Units

Savings-surplus units are net suppliers of funds to financial markets. The word net is critical because most economic units participate on both sides of financial markets. That is, they both demand and supply funds. A household, for example, may issue a mortgage to purchase a home and, during the same period of time, add to its demand or saving deposit balances at a commercial bank. Savings-surplus units are net suppliers because they supply more funds than they demand.

Each individual economic unit disposes of its income (Y) in the form of consumption expenditures (C), purchases of capital goods (I), or in the net accumulation of financial assets (Δ FA). If Δ FA > 0, the unit is purchasing more financial instruments (stocks and bonds) than it is issuing. The opposite is true when Δ FA < 0. This disposition of income for the economic unit is formally stated in 2.2).

2.2) $\quad Y = C + I + \Delta FA$

2.3) $\quad Y - C = S = I + \Delta FA$

Saving for an economic unit is the abstinence from consumption, or Y – C. As is apparent in 2.3), saving can assume two different forms. Real saving occurs in the form of capital goods purchases. In a world with no financial markets, this is the only form of saving. (With no stocks and bonds, Δ FA = 0 for every economic unit.) Financial saving, by contrast, occurs through the purchase of financial instruments.

As a net supplier of funds to financial markets, Δ FA > 0 for a savings-surplus unit. The unit shows a net accumulation of financial assets, as shown in 2.4). With income for the unit exceeding its expenditure on both consumer and capital goods, what is left over assumes the form of a net accumulation of financial assets.

$$2.4) \quad Y - C - I = \Delta FA > 0$$

$$2.5) \quad Y - C = S > I$$

Equation 2.5) is the result when one transposes investment (I) to the right-hand side of the inequality in 2.4). This is a more common way of expressing the position of the savings-surplus unit. Savings of the unit exceeds investment for the unit.

ii)   Savings-Deficit Unit

Savings-deficit units are net demanders of funds in financial markets. Their income is less than expenditures for consumer and capital goods. The position of this unit is presented symbolically in 2.6). In order to spend more than their income, these units become net issuers of financial instruments. In doing so, they demand funds in the financial marketplace.

Again, the more common way to describe the position of a savings-deficit unit is 2.7). Saving for the unit is less its purchase of capital goods (I).

$$2.6) \quad Y - C - I = \Delta FA < 0$$

$$2.7) \quad Y - C = S < I$$

While an individual economic agent may be either a savings-surplus or savings-deficit unit, it is not possible for such positions to hold in the aggregate. The reason is that whenever someone issues a financial instrument, someone else purchases that instrument. Aggregation across all units produces a wash. That is, the net change in financial assets for all economic units (viewed collectively) is zero, i.e., $\Delta FA = 0$. If that is the case, then all aggregate saving is in the form of real saving ($S \equiv I$). These aggregate relationships are shown in equations 2.8) and 2.9).

$$2.8) \quad \sum_i (Y - C - I)_i \equiv 0, \text{ and}$$

$$2.9) \quad \sum_i (Y - C)_i \equiv \sum_i S_i \equiv \sum_i I_i \qquad i = (1,2,3,4,\ldots\ldots,n)$$

B. Financial Flows

Net financial flows through markets are from savings-surplus units (SSU) to savings-deficit units (SDU). The term net is significant because nearly all economic units participate on both sides of the financial marketplace. Households are the major savings-surplus units. Businesses and governments are the primary savings-deficit units. In a very general sense, then, financial flows are from the household sector to the business and government sectors of the economy.

These financial flows are depicted in FIGURE 2.2. They are referred to as direct finance if the flow from savings-surplus units to savings-deficit units does not involve financial intermediation. Without intermediation, the savings-surplus units actually purchase the securities issued by savings-deficit units. Such exchanges do not preclude the brokerage function. That is, a broker may bring these savings-surplus and savings-deficit units together.

Direct finance occurs, for example, when a household or business purchases a U.S. Treasury-bill at the weekly T-bill auction (on Mondays). In this case, the U.S

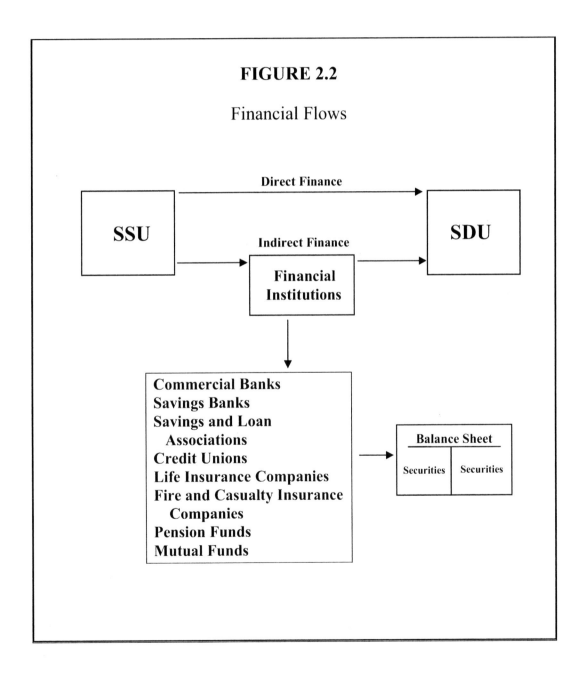

FIGURE 2.2

Financial Flows

government is a savings-deficit unit. It is issuing Treasury-bills to finance deficit spending by the Federal government. Households and businesses purchasing T-bills are savings-surplus units (so long as they are net suppliers of funds to financial markets). Because these auctions occur at Federal Reserve Banks, these Reserve Banks are performing the brokerage function.

A second example involves the sale of newly issued bonds by a utility company. Households may purchase some of these bonds from a stock-brokerage firm that is providing brokerage services. It is direct finance because these households are purchasing securities issued by a savings-deficit unit (the utility company). Again, households making such purchases are classified as savings-surplus units if they are net suppliers of funds to financial markets.

Financial flows are described as indirect finance if there is financial intermediation. Intermediation occurs when funds pass through financial institutions. What distinguishes these institutions from other businesses is that securities dominate both sides of their balance sheet. They issue securities, which appear on the right-hand (or liability) side of their balance sheet. Funds obtained from selling these securities are then employed to purchase securities for the left-hand (or asset) side of their balance sheet.

If financial institutions are to operate with a profit, they must have a positive spread. The spread is the difference between two balance-sheet rates. It is the average rate that a financial institution earns on the securities they own (from the left-hand side of the balance sheet) minus the average rate that pay on debt securities that they issue (from the right-hand side of their balance sheet). For example, if the average return on a bank's assets is 5 percent and the average cost of its liabilities is 4 percent, the spread is one percent. Spread must be positive for a financial institution to be viable.

This raises an interesting issue. For a financial institution to operate successfully, it is apparent from FIGURE 2.2 that it must intercept the flow of funds from savings-surplus units to savings-deficit units. To operate with a positive spread, however, the financial institution must offer savings-surplus units a lower rate (on average) than they would obtain if they opted, instead, to purchase securities directly from savings-deficit units. The question, then, is: why would savings-surplus agree to this arrangement?

The answer to this question provides insight into the operations of financial intermediaries. To induce savings-surplus units to purchase their securities with a lower average return, financial institutions must design financial instruments with features that are attractive to market participants, and that also are not present in the instruments (stocks and bonds) offered by savings-deficit units. Investors must view these features favorably enough to cause them to purchase the securities offered by financial institutions with the lower return. The growth and proliferation of financial institutions during the past half-century is a testimony to their ability to accomplish this.

The innovative features in the instruments offered by financial institutions are varied. Some provide customers with favorable denominations. This is particularly true of depository institutions, where customers are able to deposit sums that vary anywhere from a few dollars to millions of dollars. Liquidity, too, is an important feature, and depository institutions also offer instruments that are used as exchange media.

Many of the instruments offered by financial institutions allow owners to reduce their risk exposure. Deposits offered by banking institutions, for example, frequently carry insurance against default risk. Investment companies (or mutual funds) permit share owners to participate in the returns on a broadly diversified portfolio of securities. Life insurance companies offer securities with death benefits.

II. Intertemporal Production and Exchange

The interest rate falls within the realm of intertemporal economics, or what Austrian theorist Eugen von Böhm-Bawerk called the "the present and future in economic life."[9]   While the interest rate is not defined by everyone in the same way, it is useful to observe that the interest rate is intimately related to three intertemporal economic relationships: 1) the marginal productivity of capital; 2) the price of credit; and, 3) the marginal rate of time preference. Each of these phenomena has been employed in formulating a definition of the rate of interest. Hence, selection of language for describing these intertemporal relationships is central to the problem of defining the interest rate.

A. Marginal Productivity of Capital

Unlike land and labor, capital goods are the produced means of production. Moreover, they are produced for good reason. The production and use of capital goods, while necessarily more time-consuming (or "roundabout" according to Böhm-Bawerk), generally is productive. That is, the use of previously produced goods to produce

---

[9] Böhm-Bawerk, Eugen von. *Capital and Interest*, vol. I-III (South Holland, Ilinois: Libertarian Press), 1959. This translation and compilation is from Böhm-Bawerk's books on capital and interest written from 1884-1914. Chapter I in Book IV of Volume II is entitled "Present and Future in Economic Life."

additional goods generally results a net increase in the quantity of these goods. This net product, at the margin, is called the marginal productivity of capital MP_K.

The productivity of capital goods raises the issue of how to describe this net product that results from their usage. Böhm-Bawerk referred to it as interest or, more specifically, originary interest. Interest in this sense is the payment to the input capital. Unless it is placed in the context of the intertemporal valuation of goods, however, this payment is likely to vanish (or go to zero). If individuals make no distinction (or are indifferent) between an equal quantity of goods now or goods in the future, they will tend to accumulate capital goods currently until the marginal product of capital is zero. At that point, capital accumulation ceases and the interest rate is zero.

B. Price of Credit

Individuals can give up their claims on current goods to others, and receive in exchange claims on future goods. Contracts specifying such exchanges are loan contracts, or bonds. The excess of future goods (if any) resulting from this intertemporal exchange is also commonly called interest (or the interest rate when expressed in proportionate terms).[10]

Borrowers who issue these bonds are renting the use of money for a specified period of time. Thus, when used in this context, the interest rate is a rental payment for the use of borrowed funds. This rate is frequently described, alternatively, as the price of credit.

---

[10] Böhm-Bawerk referred to this as contract or loan interest. Irving Fisher also defined interest in this manner. Fisher, Irving, *The Theory of Interest* (New York: Augustus M. Kelley), [1930] 1961.

The price of credit, likewise, will tend to vanish unless it is placed in the context of the intertemporal valuation of goods. If individuals make no distinction (or are indifferent) between an equal quantity of goods now or goods in the future, they will readily exchange present and future goods with one another on equal terms. The price of credit in this case is zero.[11]

C. Marginal Rate of Time Preference

The phenomenon that keeps the marginal productivity of capital and the price of credit from potentially going to zero is time preferences. These subjective preferences represent how individuals value goods now relative to goods in the future, or present consumption relative to future consumption.

The marginal rate of time preference (MRTP) is a quantitative expression of these valuations for incremental units. It is the quantity of future goods an individual is willing to sacrifice for a specified quantity of present goods of comparable quality. It normally is formulated in proportionate terms, as in 2.10). If MRTP = 5%, for example, an individual is indifferent between a given quantity of present goods and five percent more future goods.

$$2.10) \quad MRTP = |dC_1 / dC_0| - 1,$$

where dC_1 and dC_0 are changes in future goods (or consumption) and present goods respectively. The ratio of these changes is an absolute value.

---

[11] This analysis abstracts from other factors that might make for a positive price of credit even if individuals are indifferent between goods now and goods in the future. They would include transaction costs and risk. The issue of risk is discussed in some detail below.

An individual who prefers present goods over future goods is said to have positive time preferences, i.e., MRTP > 0. One who is indifferent has neutral time preferences (MRTP = 0), and one who prefers future goods over present goods, negative time preferences (MRTP < 0).

Individuals are generally viewed as having positive time references. If that is the case, then the marginal productivity of capital and the price of credit need not vanish. The case of a positive price for credit (or interest) is considered below in the discussion of the real interest rate. The case for a positive marginal productivity of capital is discussed presently.

In the absence of a credit market, all capital formation is internally financed. That is, all capital goods are financed through the saving of the economic unit accumulating capital goods. Each unit must weigh the value of current goods sacrificed against the value of the additional future goods resulting from the employment of those capital goods. With positive time preferences, the unit will accumulate capital goods (currently) up to the point where the marginal productivity of capital is equal to the marginal rate of time preference.

2.11) $MP_K = MRTP > 0$

If the marginal productivity of capital were to exceed the marginal rate of time preference ($MP_K > MRTP$), the individual will choose to further abstain from present consumption and accumulate more capital goods. Assume for example that the MP_K is six-percent and the MRTP is five- percent. This individual would be indifferent between

41

a given quantity of present goods and five-percent more future goods. However, abstaining from this quantity of present goods (and accumulating additional goods) results in six-percent more future goods. The individual is clearly better off accumulating more capital goods, and will continue to do so until equality 2.11) obtains. By similar reasoning, the individual will accumulate fewer capital goods whenever the marginal productivity of capital is less than the marginal rate of time preference, again until 2.11) obtains. It is important to note that, in both of these cases, positive time preferences result in a positive marginal productivity of capital.

D. Defining Interest

While there is general agreement concerning the intertemporal nature of interest, there is no such general agreement about the definition of the interest rate. It has been defined as the return to the input capital and, alternatively, as the price of credit. Ludwig von Mises defined it yet another way: as the rate of time preference.[12]

There is good reason for defining interest in this manner. It was noted above that both the return to capital and the price of credit tend to vanish (or go to zero) in the absence of positive time preferences. That is, both of these phenomena rest on the pillars of time preference. They are simply different manifestations of the terms on which individuals are willing to exchange future goods against present goods.

For that reason, the interest rate is defined as the rate of time preference. When defined in this manner, the interest rate is often called the "pure rate of interest." It

---

[12] Mises, Ludwig von, *Human Action: A Treatise on Economics*, 3rd rev. edition, San Francisco: Fox and Wilkes, [1949] 1966.

    A well known student of von Mises, Murray Rothbard, defined interest in the same way. See Murray Rothbard, *Man, Economy and State: A Treatise on Economic Principles*, (Princeton, New Jersey: D. Van Nostrand), Volume 1, 1962.

involves the willingness to exchange a *certain* quantity of future goods for a *certain* quantity of present goods. Other factors can potentially affect this exchange rate, and are considered below. For example, if the quantity of future goods received becomes uncertain, risk enters into exchange rate of present goods against future goods.

Viewed as the marginal rate of time preference, the interest rate term is general enough to encompass both credit transactions and the return to capital (and resources more generally) when applied in the production process. It is within the narrow context of credit transactions that the term interest rate is subsequently employed. The motive is expediency. Most often the interest rate term is used in reference to the price of credit. This is particularly true in considerations of money and monetary policy.

III. Interest Rates

A. The Real Interest Rate

The interest rate can be expressed either in nominal or real terms. The nominal (or money) interest rate is the price of credit expressed in terms of money. The real interest rate is the price of credit expressed in terms of physical units (or goods and services).

When markets are free, borrowers and lenders determine the price of credit. It is anticipated that these economic agents will act rationally, i.e., that they will think in real terms. (Those who do not are said to suffer from "money illusion.") It follows that, for such rational decision-makers, it is the real interest rate that influences their choices.

43

This makes the analysis of credit markets somewhat subtle, because the real interest rate generally is not observable. What we typically observe is the nominal rate of interest. The nominal rate is the one typically quoted in the financial media, and it generally is the rate explicitly negotiated in credit contracts. This means that economic agents think in real terms, but most often negotiate credit contracts in nominal terms.

i) The Positive Real Rate of Interest

With few exceptions, those who attempt to estimate the real interest rate obtain a positive number. A fundamental analytical issue, then, is explaining this empirical outcome---that the real rate of interest is positive. The theory advanced to account for this phenomenon is the existence of positive time preferences for consumption. As noted above, time preferences are concerned with how individuals value goods now relative to an equivalent amount of goods in the future (or present consumption relative to future consumption). An individual who prefers present consumption to future consumption is said to have positive time preferences. By contrast, one who is indifferent has neutral time preferences; one who prefers future consumption, negative time preferences.

If a sufficient number of individuals have zero time preferences, the real interest rate will be zero. Those who wish to borrow in the credit market are able to obtain additional claims on current goods from lenders with zero time preferences. These lenders are indifferent between current consumption and future consumption, and willingly give up their claims to current goods in exchange for claims to future goods. Moreover, they do so at a zero interest rate. Compensation in the form of a positive real interest rate is unnecessary because of their indifference between present and future consumption.

This is shown graphically in FIGURE 2.3. The supply curve for loanable funds follows the quantity axis. No matter what the demand for loanable funds, the real interest rate remains zero. Graphically, as the demand for loanable funds shifts from D_0 to D_1 to D_2, the supply of funds is perfectly elastic at the zero rate of interest.

On the other hand, if a significant number of individuals have positive time preferences, the real interest rate will be positive. Now, individuals borrowing (in the credit market) to acquire more current goods must pay a positive real interest rate. The reason is that lenders with positive time preferences will not give up their claims on

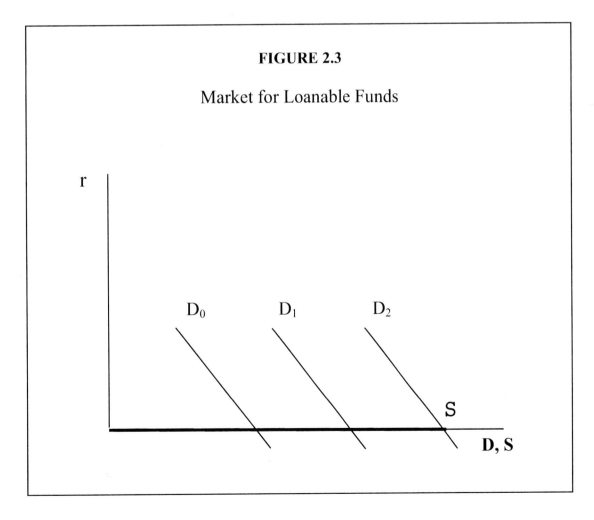

FIGURE 2.3

Market for Loanable Funds

current goods unless they are compensated.

It is in this way that positive time preferences account for the existence of a positive real interest rate. Moreover, this real rate is a precise expression of those time preferences. Hence, the real interest rate is referred to as the rate of time preference. A 5 percent real interest rate, for example, indicates that individuals are willing sacrifice present consumption if they are compensated by 5 percent additional future consumption.

ii) Level of the Real Interest Rate

A graph of the loanable funds market is presented in FIGURE 2.4. Both sides of the market reflect the time preferences of market participants. The supply curve shows quantity of loanable funds supplied at each real interest rate. These loanable funds

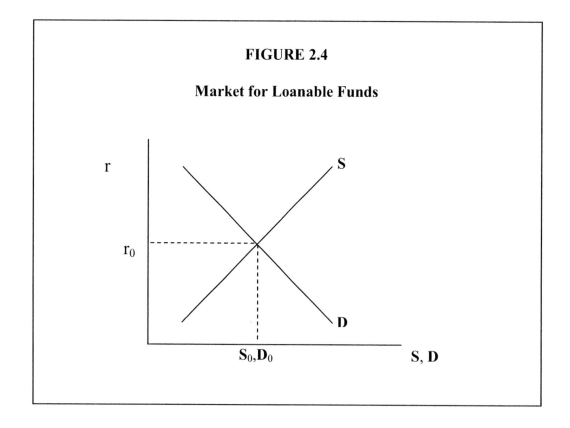

FIGURE 2.4

Market for Loanable Funds

represent claims on present consumption that economic agents are willing to forego. A higher real interest rate represents a larger compensation for deferring present consumption. Consequently, more funds are supplied at higher real interest rates.

The demand side of the market for loanable funds also reflects time preferences. Borrowers in this market obtain claims for present consumption from lenders. Some borrowers may be consumers desirous of consuming in excess of their income, i.e., dissaving. Others may be businesses wanting to finance the acquisition of additional capital goods by borrowing.

Borrowers must sacrifice future consumption in order to obtain claims for present consumption. The amount of the sacrifice is specified by the real rate of interest, which indicates the rate of exchange of future consumption for present consumption. With a smaller sacrifice (i.e., the lower the real interest rate), more funds are demanded by borrowers.

Price plays an allocative role in this market. The real interest rate allocates available funds among alternative users. At the equilibrium interest rate, r_0, the quantity of loanable funds demanded is equal to the quantity supplied. The disparate plans of all market participants are rendered consistent with one another. It is adjustments in the real interest rate that brings about this consistency of plans.

When the plans of all economic agents are consistent with one another (at interest rate r_0), resources in the economy are allocated in such a manner that aggregate saving is equal to aggregate investment ($S = I$). All resources released by those abstaining from present consumption are absorbed in the production of capital goods. These capital goods, in turn, are available for the future production of consumables.

As an expression of time preferences, the real interest rate is the market assessment of how economic agents are willing to exchange present and future consumption. When these time preferences change, so, too, does the real interest rate. Assume, for example, that there are reduced time preferences for present consumption. This can take several forms. Some individuals with positive saving may choose to save more. The result is a rightward shift in the supply curve of loanable funds (from S_0 to S_1 in FIGURE 2.5, panel a).

Another possibility is that individuals previously dissaving choose to dissave less. In this case, the demand for loanable funds decreases and the demand curve shifts to the left (from D_0 to D_1 in panel a). A third possibility is that there is a combination of the two. That is what is depicted in FIGURE 2.5, panel a). The supply of loanable funds increases and the demand decreases. At the previously prevailing interest rate (r_0), there is now an excess supply of loanable funds. Competition among suppliers results in a decline in the equilibrium real interest rate. The new market clearing rate is r_1.

Changes in the perceived marginal productivity of capital also cause time preferences to change. An increase in the productivity of capital, for example, increases business demand for capital goods. Capital goods are present goods, and this constitute an increase in time preferences for current goods. This results in an increase in the demand for loanable funds. In FIGURE 2.5, panel b), the demand curve for loanble funds shifts to the right (from D_0 to D_1). At the previously-prevailing real interest rate, r_0, there is now excess demand for loanable funds. Competition among those seeking claims to current consumption forces the real interest rate upward. The market clears at interest rate r_1.

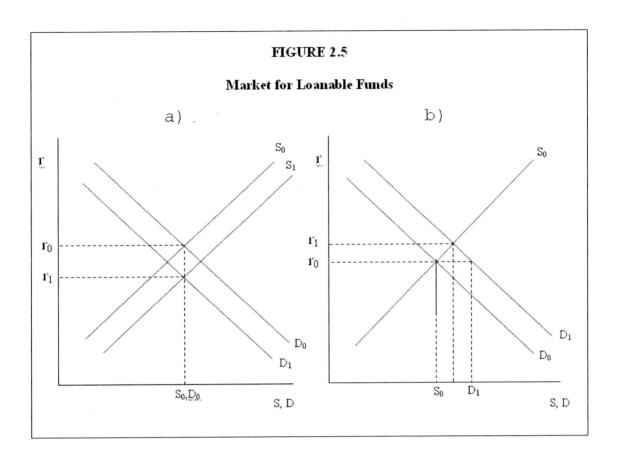

FIGURE 2.5

Market for Loanable Funds

iii) Risk and the Real Rate of Interest

Analysis of the real interest rate to this point has neglected risk factors.[13] The "pure" interest rate was a risk-free rate. The introduction of risk can affect the level of the real interest rate because risk-averse lenders must be compensated for the risk that they incur as suppliers of funds to financial markets.

There are several types of potential risk that are of importance to market participants. Two are default risk and price risk. Default risk is the risk that the borrower will not repay funds that are advanced by lenders. If that occurs, the lender incurs

---

[13] Transactions costs, which are not discussed here, are also neglected. They, too, can affect the level of the real interest rate.

49

financial loss. Given this possibility, borrowers generally must compensate lenders by offering a risk premium in the real rate.

Price risk, on the other hand, is the risk that the price of a debt security will vary during the holding period. It has significance to investors because they often do not know with certainty when the security will be liquidated. Selling a security whose price has fallen substantially results in a sizable capital loss. As a consequence, this type of risk, too, can give rise to a risk premium in the real interest rate.

The size of the risk premium, if any, in the real interest rate is dependent upon the risk preferences of market participants. For those who are risk-averse, less risk is preferred to more risk. If investors generally exhibit such preferences, the real rate will include a risk premium that embodies the market valuation of the risk involved.[14] Greater risk is associated with a higher risk premium (and a higher real interest rate); lower risk, with a lower risk premium (and real rate).

Although we are unable to directly observe the preferences of market participants, rate patterns in the marketplace generally are consistent with risk-averse behavior as described above. The dominance of this type of behavior has significance beyond affecting the level of the real interest rate. With risk-averse behavior, the real interest rate no longer represents the rate of time preference for both borrowers and lenders. There is now a wedge between those time preferences in the amount of the risk premium.

This situation is shown graphically in FIGURE 2.6, where the loanable funds market in the presence of risk is compared to the same market when there is no risk. Consider, initially, the case with no risk. The supply and demand for loanable funds are represented by curves **S** and **D** respectively. With price playing its customary rationing

---

[14] No risk premium is necessary if investors are generally risk-neutral or risk-preferred.

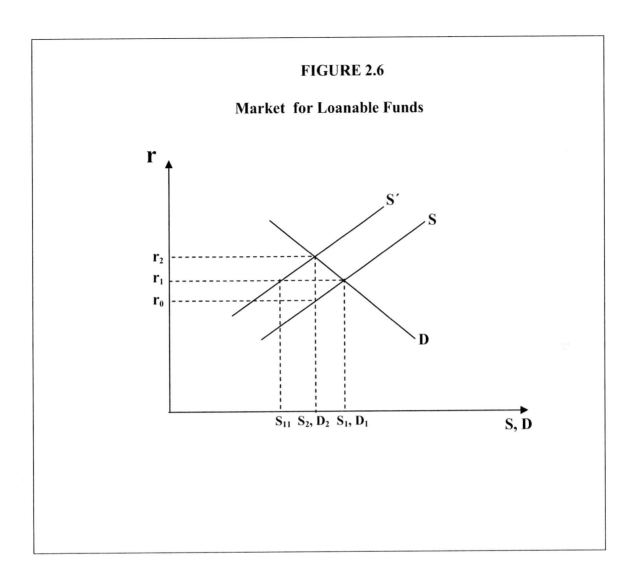

FIGURE 2.6

Market for Loanable Funds

role, the loanable funds market clears at interest rate r_1. This real interest rate represents

the time preferences of both lenders and borrowers. At this rate, the quantity demanded

of loanable funds (D_1) is equal to the quantity supplied (S_1).

Once risk is introduced, risk-averse investors will require compensation for the

risk they incur. Compensation occurs because they are less willing to lend than they were before. This is manifested in a leftward shift in the supply curve for loanable (from S to S′). For each quantity of loanable funds supplied, the real interest rate is now higher. At the previous equilibrium interest rate (r_1), there is now an excess demand for loanable funds ($D_1 - S_{11}$). Competition among borrowers drives the real rate higher to its new equilibrium level, r_2. The quantities of loanable funds supplied and demanded are now S_2 and D_2.

This new equilibrium interest rate (r_2) is an expression of the time preferences of borrowers. It represents how much future consumption they are willing to sacrifice in order to consume more currently. r_2, however, does not represent the time preferences of lenders. Instead, it represents the summation of the time preferences of lenders (r_0) and the necessary risk premium ($r_2 - r_0$) given their risk-averse behavior.

In the absence of risk, lenders will supply a lower quantity of funds, S_2, at rate r_0 (a movement down supply curve **S**) than they would at r_1. The rate r_0 now represents their tradeoff of present and future consumption, or their time preferences. In the presence of risk, a risk premium ($r_2 - r_0$) is added to their rate of time preference, and lenders supply the same quantity of funds, S_2, at the higher real rate r_2. The risk premium now constitutes a wedge between the time preferences of borrowers and lenders.

B. The Nominal Interest Rate

The nominal interest rate is the price of credit expressed in monetary units. Most interest rate quotes are nominal rates. There are number of important features relating to the nominal rate of interest. The nominal interest rate is related to bond prices, and it is also affected by inflationary expectations. Given that the characteristics of bonds can vary, there is not a single nominal rate. Instead there are many different nominal interest rates.

i) Bond Prices and Interest Rates

Bonds traded in financial markets represent borrowed funds. They are issued by borrowers and purchased by lenders. Associated with each bond is a price and an interest rate. Bond prices are an expression of the subjective value of the bonds to traders in the market. These valuations change and, as a consequence, so do bond prices.

Those issuing bonds usually are renting the use of money for a specified period of time. The rental payment for these funds is the interest rate. Thus, the interest rate is the price of credit. Having stated this, it is important to state what the interest rate is not. The interest rate is not the price of money, as is sometimes claimed. The price of money, as noted above, is its exchange value relative to other things. Assuming that P is the average price of other things, then the purchasing power of money (or the price of money) is the reciprocal of P. (Refer to equation 1.10 above.)

Many bonds are actively traded in the secondary (or resale) market. In the secondary market, bond prices and nominal (or money) interest rates are inversely related. This occurs because the nominal interest rate for newly issued (or primary) debt constantly changes. Market traders respond to variations in the interest rate by revaluing previously issued bonds. This revaluation is necessary for previously issued debt securities to remain price-competitive with the newly issued debt.

An example of this kind of revaluation is presented in EXHIBIT 2.1. The bond traded is a perpetuity, i.e., it has no maturation date. The borrower issues the bond in

EXHIBIT 2.1

Bond Prices and Interest Rates

Period	Bond Price	Coupon	Interest
1	$1,000	$50	5%
2	$500	$50	10%

period 1 with a price of $1,000. The coupon payment of $50 is sufficient to induce lenders to purchase the bond. With this coupon payment, the bond owners receive 5 percent nominal interest on this investment.

In period 2, market conditions change. The nominal interest rate on newly issued debt increases to 10 percent. The individuals who purchased the perpetuity in period 1 continue to receive an annual interest (or coupon) payment of $50. If they choose to sell their bonds in period 2, however, they will have to do so at a lower price. No one will pay them the $1,000 they initially paid for the bonds. At that price, those purchasing these perpetuities would only receive an interest rate of 5 percent. This is below the 10 percent rate they would receive when purchasing newly issued debt securities.

However, investors would be willing to purchase these perpetuities on the secondary market at a lower price. At a price of $500, the interest rate they would receive when purchasing these securities on the secondary market is equal to the 10 percent return on newly issued bonds. That is, $50/$500 = 10%.

This example was for an increase in the nominal interest rate. If the nominal rate were to fall, the opposite occurs. Bond prices increase. In general, when the nominal interest rate changes in financial markets, prices of previously issued bonds in those markets move in the opposite direction.

ii) Inflationary Expectations

Study of the relationship between the nominal and real rates of interest usually draws upon the analysis of Irving Fisher. According to Fisher, it is possible that the two rates could be the same. However, they differ from one another in an inflationary environment. Because the world of fiat money is a world of inflation, Fisher's analysis of interest rates has assumed considerable importance in the study of credit markets.

Equation 2.12) below is known as the Fisher Equation. It shows the relationship between nominal and real rates of interest, and how they are affected by inflation.

2.12) $i = r + (dP/P)^*,$

> where i is the nominal interest,
> r is the real interest rate,
> and (dP/P)* is the expected rate of change
> of the average price during the term of
> the credit contract.

Credit contracts are *ex ante* relationships. Any inflation that occurs during the term of the contract will erode the purchasing power of the money loaned. Borrowers will repay lenders in monetary units that have less purchasing power than the money initially loaned. This affects the real wealth of both borrowers and lenders. As a consequence, rational economic agents (on both sides of the contract) will take inflation into account when entering credit contracts.

When credit contracts are consummated, the actual rate of inflation during the term of a contract is not known. What affects contracts, then, are the inflationary expectations of borrowers and lenders. According to Fisher, the expected rate of inflation $[dP/P)^*]$ is fully incorporated into terms of credit contracts---in the form of a higher nominal rate of interest. In this manner, the borrower compensates the lender for the expected change in the purchasing power of the money.

This compensation, which appears as the last term in the Fisher Equation, is known as the inflation premium in the credit contract. Note that when expected inflation goes up, so, too, does the nominal rate of interest. When inflationary expectations decline, the nominal rate falls commensurately.

Such adjustments in the nominal rate of interest are a market phenomenon. It is the way that markets accommodate inflation. Rate changes are effectuated through the activities of market participants, and occur when borrowers and lenders are free to enter into credit contracts with one another. Freedom of contracting, of course, implies the ability to negotiate price. One would not necessarily expect the same adjustment in interest rates when freedom of contracting is not permitted. This occurs when government, and not market participants, sets the price of credit.

An example of how participants in credit markets adapt to different inflationary environments is presented in EXHIBIT 2.2. In Case I, market participants expect price stability. As a consequence, the nominal and real rates are the same (3 percent). Assume Individual A lends $100 to Individual B for one year. At the end of the contract period,

EXHIBIT 2.2

The Fisher Equation

Case	i	r	$(dP/P)^*$
I	3	3	0
II	13	3	10

individual B pays Individual A $103. The payment consists of $100 in principal and $3

in interest. If inflationary expectations were correct, the $100 in principal will purchase

the same quantity of goods at both the beginning and end of the contract period.

Moreover, the $103 received by Individual A will purchase 3 percent more goods and

services than the $100 loaned. Thus, not only is the nominal rate of interest 3 percent,

but the real rate is 3 percent as well.

The world changes, and inflation increases. This affects expectations. In Case II,

borrowers and lenders now anticipate 10 percent annual inflation. These higher

inflationary expectations are incorporated into the terms of credit contracts. The nominal

rate of interest increases from 3 percent to 13 percent. The difference, of course, is the

higher inflation premium.

Now Individual A loans Individual B $100. One year later, Individual B repays

the loan with interest, or $113. Assuming expectations are correct, the $100 in principal returned will purchase 10 percent fewer goods and services than when the loan was made. The inflation premium of 10 percent, however, compensates the lender for this erosion in the purchasing power of the principal. That is, $10 of the $13 in nominal interest represents this compensation to the lender. $110 (of the $113) received by the lender will now purchase the same quantity of goods and services as the $100 initially loaned. What remains is $3 in interest. That $3 is the real interest rate in this example. The $113 received by the lender will purchase 3 percent more goods and services than the $100 initially loaned in this contract.

The same market adjustment is shown graphically in FIGURE 2.7. In the market for loanable funds, the vertical axis is the nominal interest rate; the horizontal axis, the quantity of loanable funds. Initial equilibrium occurs at the nominal interest rate i_I (or 3 percent). This corresponds to Case I in Exhibit 2.2 above. With expectations of zero inflation, the real rate of interest is also 3 percent.

In Case II, inflationary expectations increase to 10 percent. Each nominal interest rate on the vertical axis now corresponds to a lower real interest rate. For example, the 3 percent nominal rate now corresponds to a real interest rate of negative 7 percent (versus a plus 3 percent before). As a consequence, lenders will want to lend less at each nominal interest rate. Borrowers will want to borrow more at each nominal rate.

These changes appear graphically as a leftward shift in the supply curve (from S_I to S_{II}), and a rightward shift in the demand curve (from D_I to D_{II}). The previously-prevailing equilibrium rate of interest rate (3 percent) no longer clears the credit market. There is excess demand at this rate. Competition among borrowers for available funds causes the nominal rate of interest to move higher. At the 13 percent nominal rate, the

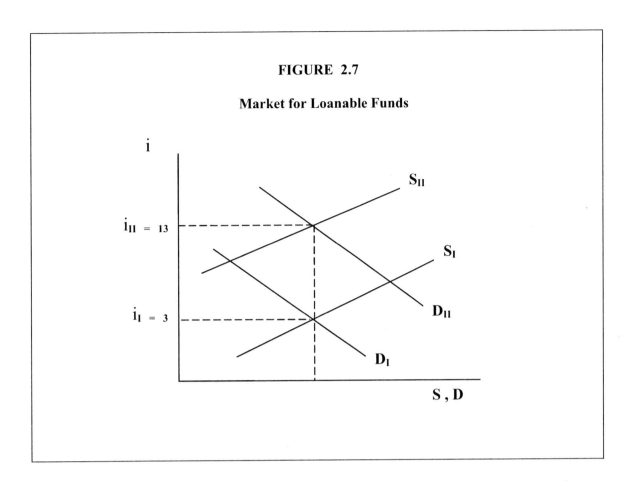

FIGURE 2.7

Market for Loanable Funds

credit market again clears. This nominal rate now corresponds to a 3 percent real interest rate. The market for loanable funds clears at the same real rate as before.

Fisher's analysis, then, shows how open credit markets accommodate inflation. Although there are numerous empirical studies of Fisher's theory, two observations are cited here to demonstrate how the theory generally conforms to the data. First, the U.S. mortgage rate recently was in the neighborhood of five percent. This is much lower than the rate in the early 1980s, which was nearly 17 percent. What would account for such a dramatic fall in the nominal rate of interest? Fisher's analysis would suggest that the inflation rate in the early 1980s must have been considerably higher. That, indeed, was the case.

A second observation is that nominal interest rates vary substantially across countries. Based on Fisher's analysis, countries with relatively low inflation should have relatively low nominal rates of interest. Alternatively, relatively high inflation countries should have correspondingly higher nominal rates of interest. That, too, generally is the case.

The final issue addressed here has to do with forecasting errors. In the previous examples, it was assumed that expectations were correct, i.e., there were no forecasting errors. In those cases, $(dP/P)^* = dP/P$. Expected inflation is equal to actual inflation or, alternatively, *ex ante* inflation is equal to *ex post* inflation.

Most often, there are forecasting errors. Such errors are important because they result in transfers of wealth. The nature of the transfer depends on whether market participants forecast the inflation rate too high or too low. When they forecast it too high $[(dP/P)^* > dP/P]$, wealth is transferred from borrowers to lenders. When $(dP/P)^* < dP/P$, the opposite occurs. Wealth is transferred from lenders to borrowers.

Examples of both types of transfer are presented in EXHIBIT 2.3. Case I is the credit contract. It is an *ex ante* relationship, with a nominal interest rate of 8 percent. The expected rate of inflation during the term of the contract is 5 percent. Given these expectations, the anticipated real rate of interest is 3 percent.

Cases II and III are two different *ex post* scenarios. In Case II, the actual rate of inflation during the term of the contract was 10 percent. This was higher than expected $[(dP/P)^* < dP/P]$. Market participants anticipated a real interest rate of 3 percent, but the

EXHIBIT 2.3

Wealth Transfers

Case	i	r	(dP/P)*	dP/P
I: *ex ante*	8	3	5	-----
II: *ex post*	8	-2	---	10
III: *ex post*	8	8	---	0

actual (*ex post*) real rate was a negative 2 percent. This unexpected lower real rate benefited borrowers at the expense of lenders. Had lenders known that the real interest rate was going to be negative 2 percent, they never would have entered the contract. Had borrowers known, they would have borrowed much more.

This forecasting error transferred wealth across the credit contract from lenders to borrowers. The form of the transfer was the lower real interest rate. Enormous amounts of wealth have been transferred in this way.

A recent historical example occurred in the U.S. in the 1970s and early 1980s. Inflation accelerated sharply. As a consequence, actual inflation rates rose above anticipated rates of inflation. While borrowers were feeling very good about long-term loan contracts consummated in the 1960s, lenders were not. Indeed, this forecasting error caused many lenders to declare bankruptcy. Among them were numerous banks and savings and loan associations. So severe was the problem that the U.S. government deemed it politically desirable to funnel large quantities of tax dollars into failing institutions.

In Case III, the actual rate of inflation (0 percent) is lower than expected inflation. This situation benefits lenders (at the expense of borrowers). The *ex ante* real interest rate was 3 percent. The *ex post* real rate was 8 percent. Many borrowers would have refused to enter credit contracts had they known the real interest rate was going to be this high.

The wealth transfer, in this case, is from borrowers to lenders. It is in the form of a higher than expected real rate of interest. The U.S. experienced this situation in the 1980s, when the rate of inflation decelerated sharply. Many borrowers declared bankruptcy. This included large numbers of farmers and building contractors.

Farmers who borrowed to acquire more land expected that land values would appreciate (as they had when inflation accelerated in the 1970s). They anticipated repaying the loans by selling commodities at higher prices (again, like the 1970s). These events did not come to pass.

A similar fate befell building contractors. Many borrowed to construct houses prior to selling them. This market tactic had "worked" for much of the 1970s. When the anticipated rise in housing prices did not materialize, expected profits turned to losses.

In a very general sense, Fisher's interest-rate model is yet another testimony to the power of markets. Through nuances in prices, markets transmit all kinds of information. In this case, the information transmitted in bond markets is the expected rate of inflation. This analysis has been especially useful in our contemporary world of fiat money, where inflation rates largely have been positive and often quite volatile. In those cases where governments have not arbitrarily fixed interest rates, Fisher's analysis shows the adaptation that occurs in financial markets in response to the vagaries of inflation.

iii) The Vector of Nominal Interest Rates

Hitherto, the discussion has focused on a single interest rate ---*the* rate of interest. That simplification facilitated discussion of the market for debt securities. In reality, there are many different interest rates. This is reflected in the interest rate vector in equation 2.13), where there are n different nominal interest rates. Individual rates in this vector might represent the interest rate on federal funds, 3-month Treasury bills, 6-month Treasury bills, 10-year Treasury bonds, corporate bonds, mortgages, 6-month certificates of deposit, and rates on numerous other debt securities.

2.13) $(i_1, i_2, i_3, i_4, i_5, \ldots i_n)$

Debt securities have different interest rates because they are not identical, i.e., they have different characteristics. Interest-rate differentials such as those in 2.13) reflect market pricing of these characteristics. Many of these characteristics were discussed above. One example is inflationary expectations and their impact on nominal interest rates. Expected inflation for the next six months may differ from expected inflation for the next two years. Both of these may differ from expected inflation for the next ten years. Because debt securities vary by maturity, the inflation premium will not be the same for securities of different maturity. This may account for a portion of the interest rate differences in equation 2.13).

Interest rates in vector 2.13) may also vary because securities do not all have the same risk characteristics. Nuances in risk are priced into securities by market participants. An example is one of the types of risk, default risk, which varies considerably across loan contracts. This reflects the fact that individual borrowers face different financial situations, and often have different ethical standards.

A case where default risk is considered relatively low is debt securities issued by the U.S. government. Like other national governments, the U.S. government has an advantage over other borrowers because it has the power to both tax and print money. Moreover, the U.S. government has a record of not defaulting on its credit contracts. As a result of these factors, market participants generally consider it very unlikely that the U.S. government will default on its debt obligations. That makes it possible for the U.S. government to borrow at relatively low nominal interest rates. By contrast, most other borrowers pay higher rates. At the other end of risk the spectrum from U.S. government securities are pay-day loans and loans at pawn shops. Default risk and interest rates are much higher for these securities.

Other factors that occasion variations in nominal interest rates include tax features and time preferences. Intergovernmental relations result in some securities having a more favorable tax status. Interest on state and local government securities, for example, generally is exempt from federal income taxes. Interest on U.S. government securities, in turn, is exempt from state income taxes. Because investors are interested in after-tax income, such differences in tax treatments are incorporated into bond prices and rates.

Time preferences have an impact because it is unlikely that the willingness of individuals to trade-off current consumption for consumption one year from now is the same as their willingness to trade-off current consumption for consumption five years, ten years, or twenty years from now. If that is the case, differences in time preferences will also account for some of the interest-rate variations observed in 2.13).

IV. The Term Structure of Interest Rates

Not only do interest rates differ at a given point in time, but returns on securities can vary based on differences in their maturity. A curve showing the yields of a set of securities differing only in maturity is known as the term structure of interest rates, or the yield curve. Each point on the curve is an ordered pair, and associates the maturity of a security with its yield. While it is not easy to find actual situations where securities differ only in their maturity, a popular rendition is to show the different yields on securities issued by the United States Treasury.

Analysis of the term structure of interest rates is related to its shape, and three yield curves with differing shapes are presented in FIGURE 2.8. The yield curve in Panel **a)** is horizontal. With a horizontal yield curve, security yields do not vary by maturity. The yield on a six-month security is the same as the yield on one-year, two-year, three-year, and ten-year securities.

The yield curve in Panel **b)** is ascending. With an ascending yield curve, the yield increases with the time to maturity. Hence, the yield on a six-month security is less than the yield on a one-year security which, in turn, is lower than the yield on a two-year security. From an empirical standpoint, the yield curve most often assumes this form. Consequently, the ascending yield curve is sometimes referred to as the normal yield curve.

The term structure depicted in Panel **c)** occurs much less frequently. Referred to as a descending yield curve, it is more likely to happen when inflation is relatively high. For a descending yield curve, the yield on a six-month security is higher than the yield on a one-year security which, in turn, is higher than the yield on a two-year security. Yields on three-year, five-year and ten-year securities are sequentially lower.[15]

A. Forward Rates

Implicit in any term structure of interest rates is a set of forward rates. These rates are not actual interest rates. Instead, they implied reinvestment rates. They are rates that would have to prevail if a sequence of investments in short-term securities is to have

---

[15] Yield curves with other shapes are also possible. Generally, they are a combination of those depicted in panels **a)**, **b)**, and **c)**. One such possibility is the humped yield curve. It initially rises, reaches a peak, and subsequently descends.

FIGURE 2.8

The Term Structure of Interest Rates

a)

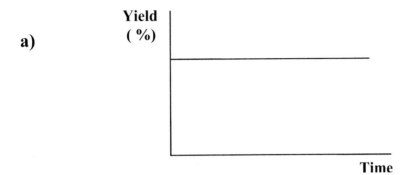

b)

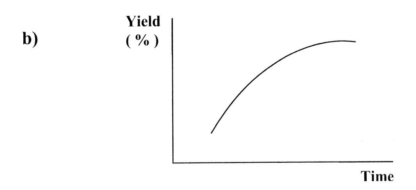

c)

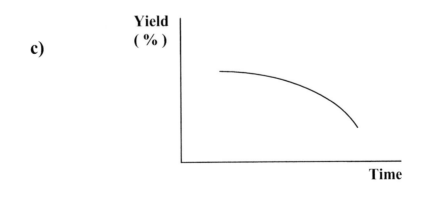

the same return as the return on a long-term security. The sum of the maturities for the short-term securities must equal the maturity of the long-term security.

Assume, for example, that bond A matures in one year and bond B matures in three years. The forward rate (in this case) is the interest rate on a two-year bond, available one year from now, that causes the compounded yield on the one year bond (A) and two-year bond to equal to the compounded yield on the three year bond (B). Thus, the proceeds from owning the one-year bond and investing the proceeds (at maturity) in the two-year bond are identical to the proceeds from owning the three-year bond. Equation 2.14) expresses this relationship symbolically.

2.14) $(1 + {_t}R_3)^3 = (1 + {_t}R_1)(1 + {_{t+1}}r_2)^2$

Where ${_t}R_3$ is the current (or spot) rate on a three-year bond,
${_t}R_1$ is the current rate on a one-year bond,
and ${_{t+1}}r_2$ is the forward rate on a two-year security
available one year from now.

Inserting numeric values, assume that the one year spot rate is four percent (${_t}R_1$ = 4%) and the three-year spot rate is five percent (${_t}R_3$ = 5%). The implicit two-year forward rate in this case is 5.504%, i.e., ${_{t+1}}r_2$ = 5.504%.

Forward rates such as this one are strictly mathematical calculations. They assume importance, however, because they are given behavioral content in explanations of the term structure of interest rates. Three alternative theories are presented below. [16] It so happens that many of the same factors employed in explaining a singular rate of interest are central to these explanations as well.

_____

[16] The following discussion of theories of the term structure draws upon James C. Van Horne, *Financial Market Rates and Flows*, 5th ed., Prentice-Hall: Englewood Cliffs, N.J., 1998.

B. Unbiased Expectations Theory

This theory relies upon expectations to account for differences in yields for securities that differ only in their maturity.[17] Each interest rate in a given term structure of interest rates is determined by expected future interest rates. Moreover, these expected future interest rates are operational. It is possible to compute them because forward rates have important informational content. According to the unbiased expectations theory, each forward rate implicit in the term structure is an unbiased estimate of the expected future interest rate for that same period.

With ρ representing the expected future interest rate, this relationship between forward rates and expected future interest rates is presented in equations 2.15) and 2.16). In 2.15), the forward rate for a j-year security available t+i years from now ($_{t+i}r_j$) is equal to the expected interest rate on the j-year security available t+i years from now ($_{t+i}\rho_j$). The unbiased nature of the forward rate is exhibited by differencing the two rates, as in 2.16).

$$2.15) \quad _{t+i}r_j = {} _{t+i}\rho_j$$

$$2.16) \quad _{t+i}r_j - {} _{t+i}\rho_j = 0$$

To further illustrate the relationship between forward rates and expected future interest rates, consider equation 2.17) below. Because all forward rates are of the form $_{t+i}r_1$, each is a one-year forward rate. According to the unbiased expectations theory, the forward rate on a one-year security available one year from now ($_{t+1}r_1$) is the estimate of

---

[17] Irving Fisher is credited with an early version of this theory. See "Appreciation and Interest," *Publications of the American Economic Association*, XI (August, 1896), pp. 23-29 and pp. 91-92.

the expected interest rate for a one-year security available one year from now ($_{t+1}\rho_1$).

$_{t+2}r_1$, in turn, serves as the estimate of the expected interest rate on a one-year bond available two years from now ($_{t+2}\rho_1$). A similar interpretation is attached to the other forward rates. It follows that the long-term rate under consideration ($_tR_n$) is determined by this set of expected future interest rates.

$$2.17) \quad (1 + {}_tR_n)^n = (1 + {}_tR_1)(1 + {}_{t+1}r_1)(1 + {}_{t+2}r_1) \dots\dots (1_{t+n-1}r_1),$$

> where $_tR_n$ is the current (or spot) interest rate on an n-year bond at time t, and $_{t+i}r_1$ is the forward rate on a one-year bond at time $t + i$.

The cogency of this argument about the nature of forward rates is not contingent upon the fact that all forward rates in 2.17) are one-year rates. Forward rates could have any maturity less than or equal to n-1. What is germane about the argument, however, is that it generalizes to all spot rates for a given term structure of interest rates. That is, each current interest rate on the yield curve is determined by expected future interest rates. That is the essence of the unbiased expectations theory.

The proposition that current interest rates are determined by expected future interest rates begs the question about determinants of expected future interest rates. The unbiased expectations theory does not address this issue, but there is little reason to believe that factors influencing future rates should differ greatly from those affecting spot rates. If that is correct, then expectations concerning time preferences for consumption and inflation loom important in explaining the shape of the yield curve. Default risk and money risk, however, largely do not. The reason is that these risk factors are generally considered a function of the maturity of a debt instrument, and maturity is not relevant to investors according to this theory of the term structure.

The unbiased expectations theory has important implications, and three are considered here. The first is an extension of the preceding discussion. The yield on a long-term bond is a geometric average of the current yield on a short-term bond and expected yields on a series of sequential short-term bonds whose maturities sum to the maturity of the long-term bond. In equation 2.17), for example, the long-term interest rate ($_tR_n$), is a geometric average of the one-year spot rate ($_tR_1$) and the expected interest rates for a sequence of n-1 one-year bonds. The maturities of these short-term bonds sum to n, the maturity of the long-term bond.

A second implication of the unbiased expectations theory is that the significance of maturity diminishes for the bond investor. If one considers an n-year investment period, the expected return is the same whether one purchases an n-year bond or a series of shorter term bonds and reinvests the proceeds. One such set of possibilities is presented in FIGURE 2.9. The compounded return with investment plan A is $(1 + {_tR_n})^n$. In this case, the investor purchases an n-year bond. For plan B, the investor purchases an n-1 year bond and invests the proceeds (at maturity) for one year. In plan C, the investor purchases an n-2 year bond and, at maturity, purchases sequentially two one-year bonds. In the final case, the investor purchases a sequential series of one-year bonds. With forward rates serving as unbiased estimates of expected future rates, the expected return for all n of these investment plans is the same. The maturity of the instruments selected has no bearing on the investor's expected n-period return.

71

FIGURE 2.9

Returns on an n-Year Investment

Investment Plan	Compounded Return
A	$(1 + {}_tR_n)^n$
B	$(1 + {}_tR_{n-1})^{n-1} (1 + {}_{t+n-1}r_1)$
C	$(1 + {}_tR_{n-2})^{n-2} (1 + {}_{t+n-2}r_1) (1 + {}_{t+n-1}r_1)$
.	
.	
.	
n	$(1 + {}_tR_1) (1 + {}_{t+1}r_1) (1 + {}_{t+2}r_1) \ldots\ldots (1 + {}_{t+n-1}r_1)$

A final implication of the unbiased expectations theory is that it provides an explanation for variously shaped yield curves. For a horizontal yield curve [as in FIGURE 2.8, panel **a)**], the level of the interest rate is not expected to change. With expected future rates the same as the current short-term rate, the average of these expected rates is identical to the current short-rate.

An ascending yield curve [FIGURE 2.8, panel **b)**] implies that bond traders expect interest rates to rise in the future. That is necessary if the geometric average of these expected future rates is above the current short-term rate. One thing that could occasion such a pattern of expected future rates is inflationary expectations, e.g., if investors expected future inflation to be higher than current inflation.

Finally, descending yield curves, which are empirically rare, occur when investors expect interest rates to fall. This normally happens when interest rates are relatively high (by historical standards). In this situation, the expectation that rates would return to more normal levels would give rise to a negatively-sloped yield curve.

One of the principal weaknesses of the unbiased expectations theory is that it assumes that transactions costs are unimportant. That is necessary if forward rates are to serve as unbiased expectations of expected future interest rates. For, if transactions costs are important, they constitute a portion of each forward rate. In this case, forward rates are higher than expected future interest rates. That is, they are (upward) biased estimates of expected future interest rates.

C. Liquidity Preference Theory

Diminution of the risks associated with bond ownership is a feature of the unbiased expectations theory. While subject to variation, both money risk and credit risk generally are viewed as positively related to the maturity of a debt instrument. This suggests that owning long-term bonds is riskier that owning short-term bonds. Given this "constitutional weakness" on the long side, the liquidity preferences of risk-averse investors will influence their portfolio selections. They will prefer to own shorter-term securities unless they are compensated for the additional risk associated with owning long-term bonds. Such considerations form the basis of the liquidity preference theory of the term structure of interest rates.[18]

If risk-averse bond traders are compensated for assuming risk, bond interest rates will contain a risk premium. Forward rates no longer are unbiased estimates of expected future interest rates. The bias in forward rates, as shown in 2.18), is in the amount of the risk (or liquidity) premium. That is, the forward rate exceeds the expected future interest rate by the amount of the liquidity premium ($_{t+i}L_j$). Alternatively, the forward rate is equal to the expected future interest rate plus the risk premium.

$$2.18) \quad _{t+i}r_j - {}_{t+i}\rho_j = {}_{t+i}L_j,$$

where $_{t+i}L_j$ is the liquidity (or risk) premium on a j-year bond available t+i years from now.

The bias in forward rates varies with the maturity of a debt instrument. Generally, the longer the maturity of an instrument, the higher is the risk premium. This reflects the fact that both default risk and money risk normally increase with the maturity of a debt instrument. If risk and maturity are strictly positively related, then the term structure of liquidity premiums is upward sloping.

$$2.19) \quad 0 < {}_{t+1}L_1 < {}_{t+2}L_1 < {}_{t+3}L_1 < \cdots \cdots < {}_{t+n}L_1$$

The presence of a term structure of liquidity premiums imparts an upward bias to the term structure of interest rates. If for, example, the expected interest rate is expected

---

[18] J. R. Hicks developed the liquidity preference argument. See J.R. Hicks, *Value and Capital*, 2nd. ed. (London: Oxford University Press, 1946), pp. 145-147.

to remain the same, the yield curve is ascending. This case is depicted in FIGURE 2.10 below.

The yield curve will also be ascending if future interest rates are expected to increase. In the case where expected interest rates are expected to fall, the shape of yield curve can be ascending, horizontal, or descending. It depends on the pattern of term structure of expected interest rates in relation to the term structure of liquidity premiums. In order to have a descending yield curve, the term structure of liquidity premiums are not of sufficient magnitude to offset a downward sloping term structure of expected

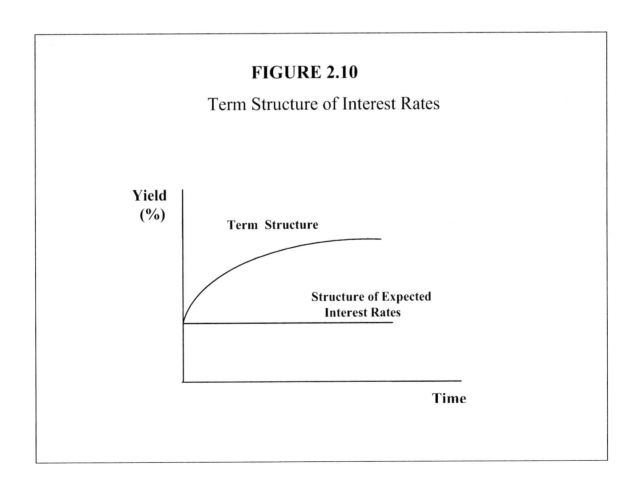

FIGURE 2.10

Term Structure of Interest Rates

interest rates.

The upward bias in the term structure under this theory is consistent with historical patterns in rates. That is, from an empirical perspective, the yield curve most often is ascending. As a consequence, an upward-sloping yield curve is frequently referred to as the normal yield curve. Dominance of the normal yield curve is precisely what one would expect under the liquidity preference theory of the term structure.

D. Market Segmentation Theory

The final theory of the term structure is the market segmentation theory. As the name suggests, markets for bonds of different maturity are completely separate, or segmented. Bonds of different maturity are not substitutes for one another at all. The rationale for such market segmentation is the risk-averse behavior of market participants. In this case, however, the concern is with income risk, rather than money or credit risk.

Income risk is the risk that relevant future income flows are subject to wide variation. One strategy for attempting to reduce this type of risk exposure is through the careful selection of bond maturities. Within the framework of segmented markets, such maturity selection assumes the form of definite maturity preferences on the part of both borrowers and lenders.

Borrowers may reduce income risk by matching the maturity of their debt issue with anticipated future cash flows. A corporation issuing a bond to finance the construction of a plant, for example, may want the maturity of that bond to coincide with the cash flow generated with its expanded production capacity. Likewise, families purchasing a home most often prefer long-term fixed-rate mortgages. That permits a better synchronization of future income flows with their debt service.

Lenders, too, may have very specific maturity preferences. Households face income risk when accumulating assets in order to finance college education for their offspring. In order to reduce that risk, they may select debt instruments whose maturities are temporally aligned with those anticipated college education expenses.

Finance institutions interested in reducing their income risk frequently do so through maturity matching. That is, they attempt to match the maturity structure of their assets with the maturity of their liabilities. Banks, with a preponderance of short and intermediate-term liabilities, may accomplish this by selecting to short and intermediate-term assets for their portfolios. If interest rates subsequently increase, both revenues and costs rise. With rate decreases, revenues and costs fall commensurately.

In contrast to banks, life insurance companies have liabilities that are long-term and somewhat predictable. Maturity matching, in their case, involves the selection of longer-term bonds. These may include corporate bonds and mortgages.

Under the strict version of the market segmentation theory, borrowers and lenders have very specific maturity preferences, and are disinclined to deviate from those preferences. Bonds of different maturity are not substitutable for one another, and the term structure is determined by the supply and demand for securities at each level of maturity. Changes in supply or demand conditions for a particular level of maturity, in turn, result in a shift in the term structure of interest rates.

A different debt-management policy by the Treasury, for example, will have an impact on the yield curve. The decision to issue a larger portion of the debt in the form of long-term bonds will increase long-term rates relative to sort-term rates. Accordingly, the slope of the yield curve increases. Similarly, more long-term corporate borrowing is expected to increase long-term rates without spilling over into shorter-term maturities.

A more moderate version of the segmented markets theory also has the term structure determined by specific maturity preferences on the part of both borrowers and lenders.[19] With somewhat less rigid preferences, market participants may be enticed to deviate from their "preferred habitat" if the inducement is sufficient. If long-term rates rise significantly relative to short-term rates, banks and other depository institutions may choose to lengthen the maturity structure of their assets. This might occur even though the maturity structure of their liabilities remains unchanged. In the absence of sizable yield inducements, however, the expectation is that market participants will adhere to their preferred maturities.

---

[19] Modigliano, Franco and Richard Sutch, "Innovations in Interest Rate Policy," *American Economic Review*, 56 (May, 1966): 178-97.

CHAPTER 3

MONEY AND FOREIGN EXCHANGE MARKETS

I.   **Foreign Exchange Markets** 80

II.   **Accounting for International Transactions** 81

        A. Digression on the U.S. Balance of Trade Deficit 85

III. **Fixed Exchange Rates: Commodity and Fiduciary Money** 86

        A. The Hume Price-Specie Flow Mechanism with
           Fiduciary Money 93

        B. Features of Fixed Exchange Rate Systems 95
           i) Domestic Monetary Autonomy 95
           ii) Economic Instability 98

IV. **Fiat Money and Fixed Exchange Rates: Government Price-Fixing in
Economically Advanced Countries---The Adjustable Peg System** 101

        A. Major Objectives of the IMF 102

        B. Problems with the Adjustable Peg 106
           i) Inconsistent Objectives 106
           ii) Adjustable Peg Not Very Adjustable..................... 110
           iii) Adjustable Peg Encouraged Speculation 113

V.   **Fiat Money and Fixed Exchange Rates: Government Price Fixing in
Less Developed Countries** 115

        A. Consequences of an Overvalued Exchange Rate 119
           i) Exchange Controls... 119
           ii) Nonconvertible Currencies................................... 121
           iii) Black Markets... 127

VI. **Fiat Money and Flexible Exchange Rates** 133

        A. Short-Run Exchange Rate Determination 133

        B. The 'Dirty Float' 140

        C. Long-Run Exchange Rate Determination:
           Purchasing Power Parity.. 144

I. Foreign Exchange Markets

There is not a single money that is used globally. As a consequence, it is necessary to exchange one money for another when engaging in international transactions. Markets where such exchanges occur are foreign exchange markets. Prices in these markets are called exchange rates, and there exists an exchange rate for each pair of currencies.[20]

Because exchanges in these markets involve trading one unit of account for another, it is customary to quote the price in terms of each of the currencies involved. For example, in the market where U.S. dollars and British pounds are exchanged, one can refer to the price of pounds in terms of dollars ($2 = 1£). Alternatively, one can express the same exchange rate as the price of dollars in terms of British pounds, i.e., 0.50£ = $1. In this respect, foreign exchange markets differ from other markets where typically only one of the two items exchanged is money (and thus a unit of account). One speaks of the price of a hat as $50, but not the price of a dollar as 1/50 of a hat.

The degree flexibility in exchange rates is dependent upon the type of money in use and the government policies toward exchange rates. The various possibilities are outlined in EXHIBIT 3.1. The types of money are those discussed in Chapter 1. Note traders (or market participants) determine the exchange rate in most cases. Government

---

[20] There is a more generic use of the term exchange rate. Whenever an exchange occurs, the number of units of one item that exchanges for a single unit of the other is referred to as an exchange rate. In the context of international financial markets, the term exchange rate assumes a much more specialized meaning.

EXHIBIT 3.1

**Exchange Rate Regimes with Different
Types of Money**

Money	Exchange Rate	Source of Pricing
I. Commodity	Fixed	Traders
II. Fiduciary	Fixed	Traders
III. Fiat A.	Flexible	Traders
B.	Fixed	Government

price-fixing becomes a potential issue with the use of fiat money. The nature of exchange rate regimes under the various types of money is the subject of this chapter. Prior to examining exchange rate regimes, however, a brief discussion of the accounting for international exchanges is undertaken.

II. Accounting for International Transactions

Because there are two sides to every transaction, the total value of things sold (S) by residents of a country must equal the total value of things bought (B) by those residents.[21] In this very general sense, then, the balance of exchanges for residents of any country will always be in balance.

$$3.1) \quad S \equiv B$$

This identity of values for things exchanged usually does not hold if one considers proper subsets of total transactions. Let us classify all exchanges as involving either goods and services (G), non-monetary financial instruments (NM), or money (M). NM is sometimes referred to as stocks and bonds.

When accounting for international transactions, it often is of interest to compare the values of goods and services sold and purchased by residents of a particular country. The difference between the value sold and the value purchased subsequently is referred to as the balance of trade (BOT) for the country. In EXHIBIT 3.2, Country A has a positive trade balance since its exports of goods and services exceed its imports. Because the overall balance of exchanges must balance, Country A must have a balance of financial instruments deficit. That is, it must import 40 more in financial instruments than it exports. In this case, the balance of trade surplus is financed by a net importation of money balances from abroad.[22]

---

[21] We are abstracting from unilateral transfers. Some countries are recipients of foreign aid, which enables them (in the aggregate) to purchase more than they sell.

[22] When we say that a country financed its balance of trade surplus by importing financial instruments, we are not suggesting that the country made a conscious decision to be a net importer of financial instruments. The basic decision-making units are individual economic agents, and the balance of payments accounting system under consideration is a consolidation of the transactions made by these units.

In a money economy, one side of every transaction is money. When we sum international transactions across economic agents, if they sell more G and NM than they buy, by definition they will be importing money balances in the aggregate.

EXHIBIT 3.2

Balance of Trade and Payments

Country A

	S	B	Difference (S - B)
(G) Goods and Services	140	100	40
(NM) Nonmonetary Financial Instruments	60	60	0
(M) Money	20	60	-20
TOTAL	220	220	0

Country B

	S	B	Difference (S - B)
(G) Goods and Services	100	140	-40
(NM) Nonmonetary Financial Instruments	60	60	0
(M) Money	60	20	40
TOTAL	220	220	0

Country C

	S	B	Difference (S - B)
(G) Goods and Services	100	140	-40
(NM) Nonmonetary Financial Instruments	80	40	40
(M) Money	40	40	0
TOTAL	220	220	0

By contrast, Countries B and C have a balance of trade deficit of 40. That is, the value of exports minus the value of imports of goods and services is equal to -40 for both countries. These countries finance their trade deficits differently. Country B finances its deficit by exporting money balances (M). Country C finances its deficit with a balance of non-monetary financial instruments surplus (NM). That is, Country C is a net exporter of stocks and bonds and, thus, does not (in the net) ship money balances abroad.

The balance of payments (BOP) position of a country is another measure of international financial flows. This figure is derived by subtracting the total value of a country's imports of both goods and services (G) and nonmonetary financial instruments (NM) from it exports of the same. For this measure, Country A has a balance of payments surplus (+ 40). Because it sells 40 more of G and NM than it purchases, it is a net importer of money balances in the amount of 40. By contrast, Country B is a net exporter of money balances because it has a balance of payments deficit for the period. The balance of payments for Country C is in balance. Its exportation of money balances to finance overseas purchases of G and NM is exactly offset by its importation of money balances that results from international sales of G and NM.

It should be clear by now that an imbalance of payments between countries gives rise to monetary shipments from the deficit country to the surplus country. Recipients of these money balances in surplus countries are owners of money balances denominated in a foreign currency. Foreign money balances generally flow to the central bank of the surplus country as their owners exchange them for domestic money at commercial banks. Commercial banks, in turn, exchange them for domestic money at the central bank. If the central bank of the surplus country chooses not to hold these money balances as international reserves, it can redeem them (for domestic money) at central banks of deficit countries. Central banks of these deficit countries lose foreign exchange holdings as a consequence of this repatriation of money balances shipped overseas.

A. Digression on the U.S. Balance of Trade Deficit

The U.S. balance of payments deficit, which has persisted for more than two decades, has received much attention. It is not uncommon for the news media to report (with dramatic undertones) that the U.S. trade deficit reached a record level the previous month. Many observers (including some economists) consider such deficits a significant problem that requires fixing---presumably by government.

While there is much drama in reporting record U.S. trade deficits, there generally is no mention of the U.S. balance of payments position. The reason is that the balance of payments tends toward zero each month. That has been the case since the U.S. adopted flexible exchange rates in the early 1970s. As is discussed in Section V. below, with a flexible exchange rate, the foreign exchange market clears and the balance of payments position goes to zero. There is, as a result, no balance of payments problem to report.

With a balance of trade deficit and a (proximate) zero balance a payments position, the aggregate accounting position for the U.S. is like that of country C above. In the aggregate, individuals in the U.S. are purchasing more goods and services from overseas sources than U.S. business are selling to those in other countries. This balance of trade deficit is financed by a balance of nonmonetary financial instruments (NM) surplus. That is, we are collectively financing our net importation of goods and services by selling economic agents in foreign countries more stocks and bonds than we are purchasing from them.

From a market-oriented perspective, it makes little sense to describe this situation as a problem. The foreign exchange market is clearing, so there is no impending crisis as there frequently is when government sets the price of foreign exchange. The millions of economic agents using the foreign exchange market have selected that combination of goods, services, stocks, and bonds that best serve their particular needs. The fact that, collectively, these choices have resulted in a U.S. has a balance of trade deficit simply means that individuals living overseas generally prefer our stocks and bonds to our goods and services.

The relative attractiveness of our stocks and bonds is not something to necessarily bemoan. It partially reflects the fact that the U.S. is a country that is both politically stable and economically free---at least, in a relative sense. As a consequence, many overseas investors feel comfortable buying financial instruments in this country.

III. Fixed Exchange Rates: Commodity and Fiduciary Money

Fixed exchange rates arise as a consequence of two quite different monetary arrangements: 1) commodity/fiduciary money standards; and, 2) fiat money with government price-fixing in foreign exchange markets. Each of these arrangements is considered.

As noted in Chapter 1, commodity money systems are characterized by the use of a money that, at the margin, has equivalent value whether used for monetary or nonmonetary purposes. For sake of exposition, assume that the money under consideration is gold. Assume, as well, that there are no fiduciary elements present in the system. This is a "pure" gold standard, with economic agents free to export and import gold.

Under such an arrangement, a given quantity of monetary gold should exchange for an equivalent amount of monetary gold. That is the basis for fixed exchange rates with a commodity money standard. In the following example, both the U.S. and the U.K are on the gold standard. The basic monetary unit in the U.S. is called the dollar. Each dollar, when minted as a coin, contains 1/20th of an ounce of gold. People in the U.K., likewise, are using gold for money. The basic monetary unit in this country, however, is called the pound, which contains 1/10th of an ounce of gold. The fixed exchange rate between the dollar and the pound under this arrangement is $2 = 1£. Only at this exchange rate will equivalent amounts of gold be exchanged for one another. Two U.S. dollars contain 1/10th ounce of gold, which is the exact gold content of one British pound.

Fixed exchange rates under a commodity money system are not a consequence of government dictum, nor are they something handed down by a deity. Instead, they result from market forces. Any deviation from this fixed rate of exchange will provide profit opportunities for traders, and their arbitrage activities will restore the 2:1 rate of exchange.[23]

---

[23] In practice, gold points about this "mint par rate of exchange" provided a trading range within which the price of gold could fluctuate without inducing arbitrage activity. These gold points reflected the costs of shipping gold from one market to another.

Consider, for example, what would happen if the market price of 1£ were $4 instead of $2. At this exchange rate, $1/5^{th}$ of an ounce of gold ($4) is exchanging for $1/10^{th}$ of an ounce of gold (1£). Gold dollars are worth more at the (British) mint than they are in the foreign exchange market. It does not require an advanced degree in economics to devise a strategy to profit from this situation. Individuals will exchange U.S. dollars for pounds at the British mint. Each pound obtained at the mint price of $2 is sold for $4 to foreign exchange dealers in the market. The $4 is then returned to the British mint and exchanged for 2£. These activities will increase (foreign exchange) dealer inventories of pounds and reduce their inventories of dollars. This provides the incentive for dealers to adjust market price in the direction of the mint price. Only when the two prices are equal will arbitrage cease.

If commodity money standards give rise to a fixed exchange rate for each pair of currencies, what assurance do we have that the fixed exchange rate will be a market clearing one? That is, how do we know that the quantity demanded will exactly equal quantity supplied at that price?

FIGURE 3.1 shows the market for the U.S. dollar in terms of British pounds. The vertical axis is the price of dollars in terms of pounds and the horizontal axis is the quantity of dollars. Economic agents demanding dollars in this market are supplying pounds. They do so in order to purchase U.S. goods and services (G) and non-monetary financial instruments (NM). Similarly, those supplying dollars are demanding pounds in order to purchase British goods, services, and non-monetary financial instruments.

In this diagram, the fixed price of 0.5 pounds per dollar is not a market clearing one. There is an excess supply of dollars in the amount of $S_1 - D_1$. An excess supply of

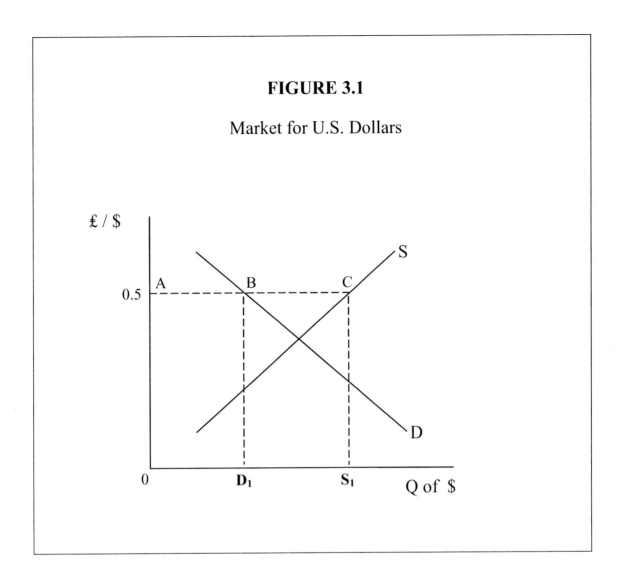

FIGURE 3.1

Market for U.S. Dollars

dollars is equivalent to saying that the U.S. is running a balance of payments deficit in its transactions with the U.K. The size of the deficit is equal to the area (D_1BCS_1).

Rectangle $OACS_1$ represents the total value (expressed in £) of dollars supplied in order to import British goods and services and non-monetary financial instruments. It is the price of dollars (0.5£/$) times the quantity of dollars supplied (S_1). The total value (expressed in £) of U.S. exports of goods and services and non-monetary financial instruments corresponds to the rectangle $OABD_1$. The U.S. balance of payments deficit is the difference in these two rectangles.

The U.S. deficit is financed by the shipment of money balances to the U.K. This raises a critical question. If individuals in the U.S. are free to export and import money balances, what will keep them from shipping the country's entire money stock to the U.K.? If this were to happen, there would be no money left in the U.S. for conducting business.

Such a prospect would appear to justify government intervention in the form of exchange controls in order to limit ability of its citizens to export money. These concerns were the basis for mercantilist policies of European monarchies, particularly in the 17th and 18th centuries. A stated objective of those policies was, indeed, to limit the outflow of a country's commodity money.

Economists credit British philosopher David Hume with developing the analysis which undermined such mercantilist thought and gave impetus to the free trade movement in 18th and 19th century Europe. According to Hume, government intervention in foreign exchange markets is unnecessary. Automatic forces of the market, in the absence of any government intrusion, will bring about equilibrium in foreign exchange markets. The equilibration process is the result of a reallocation of the world's money supply from balance of payments deficit countries to surplus countries.

The shipment of money balances from the U.S. to the U.K. in the above example changes the money stock in each country. The quantity of money now is lower in the U.S. (the deficit country) and higher in the U.K. (the surplus country). The spending of additional money balances in the U.K. results in higher prices in that country. Reduced

90

spending in the U.S. (due to a lower money supply) causes prices to fall in that country.[24]

With a fixed exchange rate, relative prices now have changed in the two countries. U.S. goods are now more price-competitive relative to British goods than they were before.

Effects of these relative-price changes on the foreign exchange market are shown in FIGURE 3.2. An increased number of individuals holding pounds now want to make purchases in the U.S. Thus, the demand curve for dollars shifts to the right (from D to

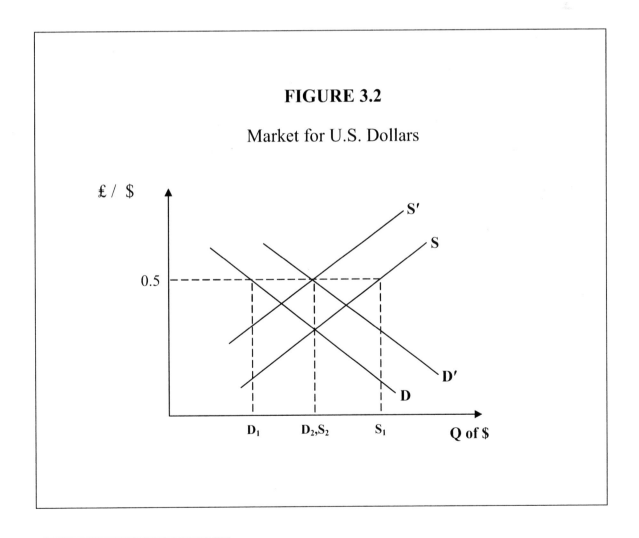

FIGURE 3.2

Market for U.S. Dollars

---

[24] This part of Hume's argument is in the quantity theory of money tradition. See Chapter 5 below.

D'). On the other hand, fewer individuals in the U.S. are interested in purchasing goods from the U.K. This causes the supply curve for dollars to shift to the left (from S to S').

The world money stock is reallocated until the U.S. balance of payments deficit disappears (simultaneously with the British surplus). At the fixed exchange rate of $0.5£ = \$1$, the quantity of dollars demanded (D_2) now is exactly equal to the quantity supplied (S_2). All of these changes occur without government intervention in the foreign exchange market, and without any change in the exchange rate. The entire adjustment is in the form of changes in both the prices of goods and services and nominal incomes in the two countries.

This compelling argument is now called the Hume price-specie flow mechanism. Adjustments under the Hume mechanism are summarized in EXHIBIT 3.3. It might be better labeled the Hume specie-flow price mechanism. Changes in money (specie-flow) ultimately bring about the changes in prices that are necessary to clear the foreign exchange market.

EXHIBIT 3.3

Adjustments Under the Hume Mechanism

| Deficit Country: | $-\Delta M \rightarrow$ | $-\Delta P$ | $\rightarrow$ | reduction in BOP deficit |
| Surplus Country: | $+\Delta M \rightarrow$ | $+\Delta P$ | $\rightarrow$ | reduction in BOP surplus |

A. The Hume Price-Specie Flow Mechanism with Fiduciary Money

When we introduce fiduciary money, Hume's argument is still valid. The situation now is different, however, since governments (as issuers of fiduciary money) can, in the short-run, either hasten or retard the adjustment mechanism of Hume.

Governments can hasten the adjustment process in the following manner. In deficit countries (which are experiencing a loss of money balances), the government reduces the quantity of fiduciary money in circulation so that the total quantity of money decreases more than it would as a consequence of financing the balance of payments deficit. In surplus countries (those experiencing monetary inflows), the central bank increases the quantity of fiduciary money. Now, the increase in the money supply is greater than it would be as a consequence of the balance of payments surplus. If governments behave in this fashion, adjustment towards balance of payments equilibrium occurs more rapidly than it would in the case of "pure" commodity money.

A more likely scenario is where government monetary policy retards the Hume adjustment mechanism. This case is more probable because governments, especially in those countries experiencing balance of payment deficits, are often tempted to offset money supply changes resulting from BOP disequilibria. When this happens, government "sterilizes" money flows. Automatic restoration of balance of payments equilibrium now occurs more slowly, and not at all in cases of perfect sterilization.

EXHIBIT 3.4 summarizes the monetary changes occurring when central banks perfectly sterilize monetary flows. In each country, government fiduciary money creation (or destruction) perfectly offsets money flows initiated by a balance of payments

EXHIBIT 3.4

Central Bank Sterilization of International Money Flows

A. Deficit Country

Change in Money Supply Resulting from BOP Deficit	-
Fiduciary Money Issue by the Central Bank	+

Net Change in the Money Supply	0

B. Surplus Country

Change in Money Supply Resulting from BOP Surplus	+
Fiduciary Money Issue by the Central Bank	-

Net Change in the Money Supply	0

disequilibrium. Because the money supply in both countries does not change, neither does the price level. Relative prices in the two countries remain unchanged, and government monetary policies have effectively neutralized the mechanism of Hume. Balance of payments disequilibria are not automatically eliminated, and deficits or surpluses persist.

There are limits to government sterilization of money flows. If a deficit country continues to increase the quantity of fiduciary money to offset the loss of specie to other countries, the ratio of commodity money to fiduciary money (G_M/FG_M) in the country declines. Long before this ratio reaches its lower limit of zero, the ability of financial institutions to convert fiduciary money into commodity money is jeopardized. Desirous of avoiding a financial panic, governments cease issuing additional fiduciary money and sterilization ceases. Hence, in the long-run, Hume's mechanism remains valid.[25]

B. Features of Fixed Exchange Rate Systems

While major trading countries abandoned fiduciary money when they went off the gold standard in the 1930s, they did not abandon fixed exchange rates. Adoption of fiat money was accompanied by government price-fixing in foreign exchange markets. Prior to examining these arrangements, two conventional arguments for leaving the gold standard are examined.

i) Domestic Monetary Autonomy

One argument was that leaving the gold standard would give individual countries greater ability to conduct an independent monetary policy. The ideas of British economist J.M. Keynes were gaining popularity at the time, and he was arguing that governments should play a more active role in stabilizing their economies.

Fiduciary money arrangements obstruct such policy activism. That is because the quantity of money in an individual country partly is a result of global economic conditions and, thus, not strictly under the control of the national monetary authority. Changes in the money supply occur not only because of changes in the domestic production of commodity money and/or the issue of fiduciary money, but also are

---

[25] A surplus country can sterilize money inflows by reducing the quantity of fiduciary money to offset specie inflows. The ratio of commodity money to fiduciary money (GM/FGM) in the country increases. Convertibility is not jeopardized. When surplus countries behave in this manner, a greater portion of the adjustment necessary to restore balance of payments equilibrium must occur in the deficit country. With perfect sterilization, all of the adjustment occurs in the deficit country.

affected by the balance of payments position of the country. Deficit countries are net exporters of money; surplus countries, net importers.

One aspect of this monetary interdependence is that individual countries are exposed to monetary shocks originating elsewhere. Assume, for example, the discovery of a rich new vein of gold in South Africa. Under a fiduciary money arrangement such as the gold standard, the increased supply of money results in higher prices in South Africa. With fixed exchange rates, South African goods become less competitive in international markets, and that country experiences a balance of payments deficit. Money flows out of the country, and inflation originating in South Africa is transmitted to the rest of the world via fixed exchange rates. These adjustments continue until monetary equilibrium is reestablished. Note that while the original monetary disturbance occurs in a single country, resolution of the disturbance is a global matter.

While fiduciary money systems are characterized by monetary interdependence, it does not follow that replacing them with fiat money necessarily will bring greater national monetary independence. Many countries adopting fiat money with fixed exchange rates discovered this. They found they simply had substituted one type of convertibility problem for another.

Use of fiat money does eliminate one convertibility problem because issuers of paper money no longer are obliged to convert that money into commodity money on demand. Individual countries, however, are not free to select the monetary policy of their choice unless, of course, that choice just happens to be consistent with the monetary policies of other countries. If it is not consistent, the country often confronts a second type of convertibility problem.

To illustrate, assume that a country chooses to issue fiat money at a much more rapid rate than do other countries. It experiences a balance of payments deficit. The money that is shipped overseas to finance the balance of payments deficit returns to the country, and depletes its foreign exchange reserves (held by the central bank). With no foreign exchange reserves, the central bank no longer can repatriate foreign-held money which it originally issued. The country now faces a second kind of convertibility problem. Refusal to repatriate its currency means that the currency becomes a nonconvertible currency, and is no longer acceptable in the international economy.[26] In addition, the country's balance of payments deficits exert pressure on the government to adopt a less expansionary monetary policy. Thus, when a country adopts a fiat money standard with fixed exchange rates, a high degree of monetary interdependence still exists.

Parenthetically, not all economists consider monetary interdependence undesirable. Critics of fiat money, such as economists in the Austrian tradition, often favorably view the constraints monetary authorities face under fiduciary standards.[27] According to them, we are much better off in a world where monetary authorities have less discretion to conduct policy. Seven decades of continuous fiat money inflation is cited as evidence of what happens when monetary authorities are given more discretion. In their judgment, only the use of fiduciary money will instill the discipline necessary for monetary authorities to limit money growth.

---

[26] For further discussion of nonconvertible currencies, refer to pages 121-127 below.

[27] Austrian economists in this tradition include Ludwig von Mises, Gottfried Haberler, and Friedrich A. Hayek.

ii) Economic Instability

A second argument against the use of fiduciary money is that it results in excessive economic instability. This argument is based upon the adjustment process delineated by Hume. Countries experiencing a balance of payment deficit finance those deficits by exporting money. Surplus countries, on the other hand, are net importers of money balances. The resulting redistribution of the world's money supply occasions adjustments in prices and nominal incomes in both deficit and surplus countries. According to critics of fiduciary money, this adjustment process generates continuous economic fluctuations which are inherent under the fiduciary money standard.

The relevant consideration, however, is not whether economic instability occurs with fiduciary money. It does. The question is whether a fiduciary money standard (such as the gold standard) is more prone to economic instability than are alternative standards. The appropriate comparison is here is with the fiat money standard.

The question is much more complex when formulated this way, and not easily resolved from an analytical perspective. Clearly two types of instability are involved--- price and income instability. The more difficult one is income instability, and it is considered first. The type of income instability of concern is variation in real output, or output measured in physical units (instead of money).

With fiduciary money (and without perfect sterilization of gold flows), balance of payments disequilibria do cause nominal income (Py) to vary. Whether changes in nominal income result in variations in real output (y) is critical. If they do not, the potential impact of BOP disequilibria on aggregate production and the employment of resources is very limited.

On the other hand, if changes in money do have a significant impact on the level of production, then adjustments to BOP disequilibria are more likely to generate business cycle fluctuations. Hence, economists who subscribe to a monetary theory of the business cycle are likely to have the greatest concern with the consequences of BOP disequilibria (and the Hume price-specie flow mechanism). Among these economists are Irving Fisher, R.G. Hawtrey, and, more recently, Milton Friedman.

The problem here is that business cycles are complex phenomena, and there is no consensus among economists concerning root causes. Only a minority of economists proffer monetary explanations. From an analytical standpoint, then, the majority of economists not accepting the monetary explanation are less likely to fret about economic instability associated with the use of fiduciary money.

Even if adjustments under fiduciary money do occasion variations in real output and employment, there is no assurance that these variations are greater than would occur with fiat money. Empirical data indicate otherwise. Variations in the money supply have been much greater since the adoption of fiat money than they were with fiduciary money. Because the perceived problem with a fiduciary money standard revolves around the instability of money, these data suggest a much greater likelihood of income instability with fiat money.

A second type of instability is price instability. The case for greater price instability under a fiduciary money standard is much weaker. Economic analysis suggests that we are likely to experience greater long-run price stability if we use commodity or fiduciary money rather than fiat money. The reason is that, with commodity or fiduciary money, there are market forces in operation that tend to bring about long-run price stability.

Consider the case of commodity money. An increase in the general price level is equivalent to a decline in the exchange value of money relative to goods and services. Because relative prices have moved in favor of goods and services, and against money, economic incentives exist for producers to employ more resources in the production of goods and services and fewer in the production of commodity money. The decline in the production of money and increase in the production of goods and services dampen the upward pressure on prices.

A similar argument holds for the case of a falling price level. Money is gaining exchange value relative to goods and services. Thus, there exist market incentives to allocate more resources the production of money. Increases in the quantity of money (and decreases in the production of goods and services) dampen the deflationary pressures.

The cogency of both of these arguments is unaffected by the introduction of fiduciary money elements into the analysis. In the short-run, it is possible for fiduciary money issue (or destruction) to neutralize (or more than neutralize) the effect of movements in relative prices on the production of commodity money. The existence of the convertibility option keeps this from happening in the case of inflation in the long-run. That option is eventually jeopardized with a continued decline in the ratio of commodity money to fiduciary money. With long-run deflation, it is also the convertibility option that limits central bank sterilization of the impact of relative price changes on the production of commodity money. In this case, the convertibility option eventually becomes irrelevant.[28]

By contrast, no such automatic market forces are present to check movements in the general price level under a fiat money standard. Elimination of the convertibility option (associated with fiduciary money) allows a central bank great freedom to change the money supply at its own discretion. With an interest in expanding the quantity of money, governments most often do. Hence, in the case of prices, use of fiduciary money is likely to result in less instability than occurs with fiat money.

IV. Fiat Money and Fixed Exchange Rates: Government Price-Fixing in Economically Advanced Countries ------The Adjustable Peg System

In addition to commodity and fiduciary monetary systems, it is also possible to have fixed exchange rates with fiat money. This occurs when exchange rates are set by government. In this case, exchange rates do not reflect the relative commodity content of different monies, nor are they the result of market trading activity. They come directly from the minds of politicians or government bureaucrats. These prices frequently are referred to as "official" exchange rates, possibly in an effort to give them legitimacy.

Government price-fixing arrangements were quite popular in the twentieth century, especially in countries with a penchant for economic planning and government regulation of the economy. Examples are found in both economically advanced countries and in less developed countries. In this section, an historical episode of government price-fixing by economically advanced countries is examined. The arrangement was

---

[28] The convertibility option is no longer relevant once the quantity of fiduciary money falls to zero.

utilized for pricing foreign exchange during much of the middle third of the twentieth century.

The adjustable peg system, as the price-fixing arrangement was called, emerged from a meeting in Bretton Woods, New Hampshire (U.S.A.) in 1944. At the time, it was apparent that World War II would end in victory by the allied countries. Economists and finance ministers of these countries were meeting to discuss institutional arrangements which would encourage an expansion of world trade in the post-World War II period. Their deliberations resulted in the formation of the International Monetary Fund (IMF) as an organization and the adjustable-peg system as a mechanism for pricing foreign exchange.

A. Major Objectives of the IMF

Founders of the IMF wished to accomplish three major objectives: 1) elimination of exchange controls; 2) national autonomy in the conduct of monetary policy; and, 3) reasonable stability of exchange rates.

Exchange controls are government imposed regulations for allocating foreign exchange. Anyone buying and selling foreign exchange must have prior governmental approval. A practical consequence is that individuals wishing to make purchases from abroad not only must have the willingness to do so, but permission from the government as well. By making it more difficult to acquire foreign exchange, exchange controls impede the flow of international trade. Removing those controls has the opposite effect. World trade increases and economic agents capture gains from trade they were unable to with exchange controls. World living standards improve.

While increased world trade was an objective of the IMF, establishing an international medium of exchange was not. Domestic monetary autonomy was deemed more important. Individual countries were expected to pursue their own national interests with regard to monetary policy. This perspective was consistent with policy proposals of British economist J.M. Keynes, who argued that an independent monetary policy was necessary if national governments were to play a more active role in attempting to stabilize their domestic economies.

The desire for "reasonable" stability of exchange rates largely was a response to the international monetary climate that prevailed during the 1930's. Relatively low levels of production and employment encouraged major trading countries to devalue their currencies in an effort to increase domestic employment at the expense of employment abroad. The problem with this strategy (of attempting to increase export demand) was that devaluation by one country frequently was met by offsetting devaluations by others. The results were perverse---disturbances to world production and trade, but little or no gain in domestic employment.

While stability of exchange rates was considered crucial, architects of the IMF were aware that some flexibility in exchange rates would, at times, be necessary. By design, then, the adjustable-peg system was a combination of fixed and flexible rates. Exchange rates were fixed, but with a mechanism for adjusting them if they were inappropriate. Founders of the IMF intended that this adjustable-peg mechanism would provide for "reasonable" stability of exchange rates.

The fixed exchange rates were established by government price-fixing in the market for a commodity with a rich monetary history---gold. Each country fixed the price of gold in terms of its money.   Setting the price of gold in this manner resulted in a

fixed exchange rate for each pair of currencies.   If, for example, the U.K. prices gold at

14£ per ounce, and the U.S. at $35 per ounce, then a fixed exchange rate exists between

the dollar and the pound: 1£ = $2.50.

As is always the case, the following question arises when government sets the price

in a market: What happens if this fixed price is not a market clearing one?   That is the

case in FIGURE 3.3, where the U.K. is running a balance of payments deficit with the

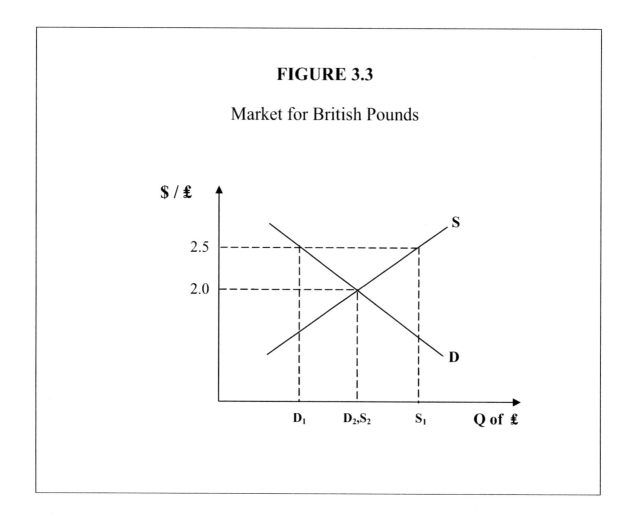

FIGURE 3.3

Market for British Pounds

U.S. At the exchange rate of $2.5 = 1£, there is an excess supply of pounds in the market $(S_1 - D_1)$. The Hume price-specie flow mechanism will not assure us of market clearing because each country is conducting an independent monetary policy. Monetary authorities may choose to offset the effects of money shipments associated with financing payments imbalances. In this situation, the central bank in the U.K. (the Bank of England) must be prepared to redeem the excess pounds British citizens are shipping overseas. In doing so, they draw upon the foreign exchange holdings of the Bank of England.

The international reserves of any central bank are finite. A problem arises when the holdings of the Bank of England approach zero in the limit. The IMF made provision for such a contingency. If the balance of payments problem was perceived as *temporary*, the U.K. was permitted to borrow reserves from the IMF.[29] The Bank of England could, in this case, use the borrowed reserves to redeem any excess pounds flowing back to the Bank as a consequence of the country's balance of payments deficit.

In situations where the balance of payments problem is considered *fundamental* (i.e., secular), a country was permitted (after consultation with the IMF) to adjust the peg. This involved changing the "official" price of gold. Deficit countries would devalue their currencies, or increase the price of gold. In the present example, the U.K. government increases the price of gold to 17.5£ per ounce. This constitutes a 25 percent devaluation of the British pound (3.5£/14£ = .25). The new fixed exchange rate between the dollar

[29] As a condition of membership, each member country of the IMF was required to subscribe a quota of gold and its domestic currency to the IMF. The gold and currencies so accumulated by the IMF were used to make loans to individual countries.

and the pound is \$2 = 1£. Since the value of the pound has fallen, people in the U.S. find British goods and services cheaper than before. The quantity demanded of pounds increases. In addition, since it now requires 0.5£ to purchase a dollar instead of 0.4£, all U.S. goods and services become more expensive for British citizens to buy; the quantity supplied of pounds decreases. In FIGURE 3.3, the new exchange rate clears the market, i.e., the U.K. balance of payments now is in balance.

B. Problems with the Adjustable Peg

This mechanism for pricing foreign exchange was operational for nearly three decades (1944-71). During that period, countries reduced barriers to international trade.[30] The volume of world trade responded by expanding significantly. Not only did post-war economies not return to the depressed economic conditions of the 1930s (as many followers of Keynes had predicted), but many countries experienced secular increases in living standards.

Despite the longevity of the adjustable-peg system, there were three serious structural flaws within the system that led to its ultimate demise: 1) the operational objectives of the system were inconsistent; 2) the adjustable peg was not very adjustable in practice; and, 3) the system encouraged massive speculation against "weak" currencies.

i) Inconsistent Objectives

While the adjustable-peg system was designed as a blend of fixed and flexible exchange rates, in practice it was essentially a system of fixed rates. The major difficulty

---

[30] In addition to the IMF, another post-war agreement contributed significantly to dismantling of trade barriers. The General Agreement on Tariffs and Trade (GATT) provided a framework for several rounds of successful negotiations. Each led to reductions in trade barriers.

with the arrangement was that the objectives of the system were inconsistent. Fixed exchange rates (objective 3) are not consistent with national autonomy in the conduct of monetary policy (objective 2). Indeed, those attempting to simultaneously accomplish objectives 2) and 3) are faced with the following dilemma. Fixed exchange rates work best when all countries follow more or less the same monetary policies. But, if all countries must follow roughly the same monetary policy, there is no national monetary autonomy.

The following example illustrates the point. Assume that two countries, the U.S. and Mexico, produce an identical product---shoes. The exchange rate between the Mexican peso and the U.S. dollar is fixed at 10p = $1 (or 1p = $.20). Moreover, assume that the initial price (in Year 0) for the shoes is the same in the two countries even though they are priced in different currencies. As shown in EXHIBIT 3.5, one can purchase the shoes in Mexico for 500 pesos or in the U.S. for $50. At these prices, consumers are indifferent between purchasing the shoes in Mexico or the U.S.

The balance of payments between the two countries also is initially in balance (point A, FIGURE 3.4). The U.S. and Mexico follow dramatically different monetary policies. The U.S. central bank, sensitive to the potential for inflation, holds the money supply constant, i.e., the annual growth rate for money is zero percent. By contrast, Mexico's monetary authorities choose to increase the money supply at a rate of 100 percent per year.

Assuming that price changes exactly mirror money growth rates, the price level will double each year in Mexico while it remains the same in the U.S. If shoe prices

EXHIBIT 3.5

Money and Price Growth in Mexico and the U.S.

Country	Annual Growth		Price of Shoes	
	M	P	Year 0	Year 1
United States	0	0	$50	$50
Mexico	100	100	500p	1,000p

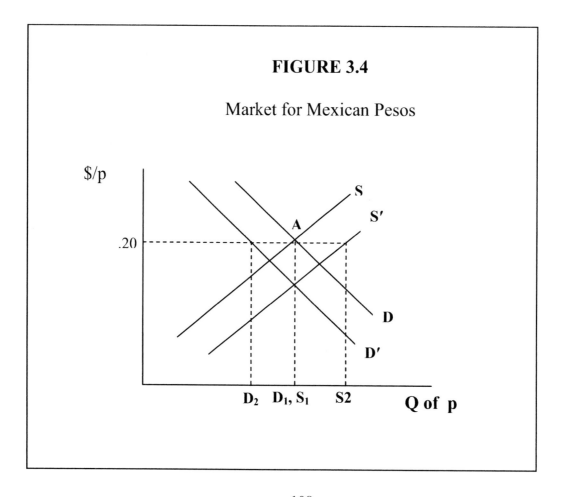

FIGURE 3.4

Market for Mexican Pesos

move in tandem with the general price level in each country, the price of shoes in Mexico in Year 1 is 1,000 pesos. They remain at $50 in the U.S. Given a fixed exchange rate, it now will be cheaper for consumers in both countries to purchase shoes in the U.S. For Americans to purchase the shoes in Mexico, the price now is $100 because that sum is required to purchase 1,000 pesos in the foreign exchange market. For Mexicans, the cost of purchasing shoes in the U.S. is 500 pesos (the cost of buying $50 in the foreign exchange market).

As a consequence of the markedly different monetary policies, producers of shoes in Mexico no longer are competitive with their U.S. counterparts. Moreover, the problem is much more general than that of selling shoes. The prices of nearly all Mexican products will have increased sharply in comparison to prices in the U.S., and consumers will prefer the relatively less expensive U.S. products in these markets as well. The result is deterioration in the balance of payments for Mexico.

In FIGURE 3.4, the supply curve for Mexican pesos shifts to the right because more Mexicans now wish to exchange pesos for U.S. dollars in order to buy U.S. products. Likewise, the demand curve for pesos shifts to the left as fewer Americans than before are interested in importing Mexican products. Rather than a payments balance, Mexico now has a balance of payments deficit in the amount of $(.20)(S_2 - D_2)$.

This balance of payments problem experienced by Mexico is the direct result of the inconsistencies of objectives 2) and 3). Fixed exchange rates are not consistent with an autonomous monetary policy in Mexico. Government officials now have a policy dilemma. They can restrict capital flows (the outflow of money) through restrictive trade policies such as exchange controls, quotas, or higher tariffs. However, this action reduces living standards by limiting the gains from trade. Alternatively, the Bank of Mexico can sacrifice its monetary autonomy by reducing its money growth rate so that it is in conformity with that of the U.S.

ii) Adjustable-Peg Not Very Adjustable

A second difficulty with the pricing mechanism of the IMF was that, in practice, the adjustable peg was not very adjustable. Indeed, use of the term adjustable peg was a misnomer. Only rarely was the peg adjusted, and that was after a balance of payments problem had reached crisis proportions.

There were two reasons for this. First, the successful implementation of the system required behavior on the part of bureaucrats which was beyond their capacity to deliver. For each balance of payments problem, they were to determine whether it was temporary or fundamental. For this distinction to be meaningful, designation of a problem as fundamental must occur prior its deterioration into a crisis situation.

This may sound simple in concept, but it is not easily accomplished. Any balance of payments position results from payments flows generated by multitudes of transactions undertaken by thousands of individuals. These individuals have differing motivations and frequently are responding to different stimuli. Forecasting their aggregate behavior is very difficult, if not impossible. Thus, it is not surprising that bureaucrats responsible for implementing the adjustable peg system were unable to make the required classifications. Because they were reluctant to classify problems as fundamental, the arrangement worked out to be one of fixed exchange rates.

Second, the adjustable peg system was designed as if it were to be carried out in a political vacuum. Nothing could be further from the truth. Those responsible for administering the system were bureaucrats and politicians. For them, the decision of whether to adjust the peg was not strictly based on economic logic, but upon political considerations as well. Prior to adjusting the peg, they must be convinced that the political benefits of such action outweigh the costs. Furthermore, this criterion must be met even when it is clear that the balance of payments problem is a fundamental one.

Hence, political factors also militated against adjusting exchange rates. To more fully understand why that is the case, it is helpful to recognize that government price-fixing in foreign exchange markets is just a special case of government price-fixing more generally. Once a government makes the decision to regulate prices, it often finds it difficult to change them.

Price inertia occurs because the pricing process has become politicized. Whenever a price changes, some individuals find themselves better off while others are worse off. If the price change occurs as a consequence of market forces, individuals who are harmed are more prone to view the situation as one where they undertook risks and the outcome was unfavorable. This is decidedly not the case once price determination is politicized. Those who are harmed by a price change know exactly why they are worse off. They are worse off because a government official decided to change the price.

Understandably, their response is political. Sometimes those harmed petition the government. Sometimes they riot in the streets. On occasion, the reaction is strong enough that governments are removed from power, either through the ballot box or in a less democratic manner. Aware of these possibilities, governments often become conservative and refuse to change the price even when economic fundamentals would dictate such action.

The situation in the U.K. during the 1960s provides an excellent example of regulatory price inertia under the adjustable peg system. After a series of balance of payments deficits, it became clear that the pound was overvalued relative to the market assessment. In the terminology of the IMF, the U.K. had a fundamental balance of payments problem. Nevertheless, the U.K. government was reluctant to adjust the peg. That reticence largely was politically based. The U.K. imported much of its food, and any devaluation of significance would sharply increase food prices. If the government were to devalue, critics (such as opposing political parties) would quickly point out that the burden of adjustment falls disproportionately upon the working classes and poor people in the country. Aware of this potential criticism, the government refused to devalue until the problem had reached crisis proportions.

In addition to the fact that exchange rate changes rearrange balance sheets, emotional elements also entered the picture. A stable exchange rate over extended periods of time was a matter of national pride. Many governments maintained that their currency was "as good as gold." The U.S. government made pronouncements of this nature in the 1950s and 1960s. It did so to assure foreign holders of dollar balances that they need not be concerned about the quality of their holdings even though the U.S. was running continuous balance of payments deficits. Those who believed such assertions found their net worth reduced when the U.S. government devalued the dollar in 1971.

iii) Adjustable Peg Encouraged Speculation

A third difficulty was that the adjustable peg system encouraged speculation against "weak" currencies, or currencies of countries with continuous balance of payments deficits and limited foreign exchange reserves. As a speculator, how would you like an institutional arrangement that permitted you to speculate in markets where there were two possible outcomes: 1) you win; and 2), you break even. This is what the adjustable peg system offered. All that was required of speculators was that they identify currencies for which there was a reasonably good chance of devaluation. This identification was not difficult. Virtually everyone had knowledge of countries with serious balance of payments problems, and whose currencies were under pressure in foreign exchange markets.

Consider again the case of the British pound with an official value of $2.50 (FIGURE 3.5). At that price, there is excess supply of pounds $(S_1 - D_1)$. Assume that the pound is a "weak" currency in the sense described above. The U.K. has borrowed heavily from the IMF, but to no avail. At the current exchange rate, borrowed reserves are quickly shipped overseas to finance the continuing balance of payments deficit. Pressure on the pound is heavy, and speculators perceive that the Bank of England is likely to devalue.

Having identified this candidate for devaluation, what do speculators do? They sell the asset they expect to decline in value (pounds) and buy the asset they expect to increase in value (dollars). Assume that a speculator sells 100,000£ in exchange for $250,000. What are the possible outcomes? One is that the Bank of England does devalue, and that the price of the dollar moves from 0.4£ to 0.5£ (the price of the £ drops

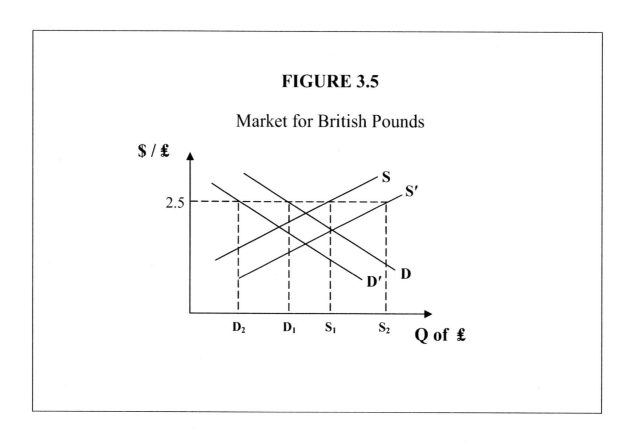

FIGURE 3.5

Market for British Pounds

from $2.50 to $2.00). Our speculator now exchanges his/her $250,000 for 125,000£, a

profit of 25,000£. If, on the other hand, the Bank of England does not devalue, the

speculator converts the $250,000 back into 100,000£. He (or she) breaks even.[31] There

is no chance that the Bank of England will revalue the £ (decrease the "official" price of

gold), which would cause our speculator to experience a loss.

Such speculative activity does make the balance of payments problem worse.

Those demanding dollars in this market are supplying pounds. As speculators reduce

pound holdings in favor dollars, the supply curve in FIGURE 3.5 shifts to the right (from

[31] We are abstracting here from transactions costs which, in percentage terms, tend to be quite small for large transactions.

S to S'). Those demanding pounds in this market are supplying dollars. In anticipation of a possible devaluation, many of these individuals delay or cancel plans to acquire pounds. As a consequence, the demand curve for pounds shifts to the left (from D to D'). The U.K. balance of payments deficit now is $S_2 - D_2$ instead of $S_1 - D_1$, i.e., the deficit is larger on account of speculative activity.

While speculative activity can aggravate a balance of payments problem, it does not follow that speculators caused the problem. This deserves mention because central bankers frequently are unwilling to admit their role in a balance of payments problem. Rather, they seek to place the blame elsewhere. Speculators are a convenient target. Thus, it is not uncommon to hear central bankers (or politicians) say: "Our nation is currently experiencing a severe balance of payments shortfall, and the underlying problem is one of excessive speculation."

To the contrary, speculators most likely play a stabilizing role in such situations. In our current example, at a price of $2.50, the British pound is overvalued relative to the price consistent with the plans of private traders. It is this price distortion which is responsible for any chaotic conditions that exist in the market. By increasing the cost of resisting devaluation, speculative activity hastens the adjustment of the exchange rate in the direction of a market clearing one.

V. Fiat Money and Fixed Exchange Rates: Government Price-Fixing in Less Developed Countries

While most major trading countries have abandoned fixed exchange rates, many less developed countries (LDCs) have not. Fixed exchange rates in these countries are not the result of actions by private traders, nor do they reflect the relative commodity content of different monies. Rather, they represent decisions made by government bureaucrats and politicians. In this respect, fixed exchange rates in less developed countries are no different from price-fixing arrangements in more highly developed countries.

One must invariably ask the following question when confronted by a fixed price in a market. What happens if the fixed price is not a market clearing one? This usually is not a significant problem when governments initially regulate prices because they often select the current market price as the regulated price. In FIGURE 3.6(a), for example, the government of Tanzania fixes the price of the U.S. dollar at 100 Tanzanian shillings (TSH). Because this is the market-clearing price, there is no balance of payments problem. The quantity of dollars supplied at this price is equal to the quantity demanded. The outcome is the same as it would be if the price were market determined.

There is little likelihood, however, that both the government-determined price and the market price will remain equal. Differences in monetary policies, for one thing, militate against it. In a world of fiat money, individual governments are free to determine the quantity of money in their country. This will not create a serious problem if money growth in Tanzania is similar to money growth in the U.S. That is not the case here. Tanzania increases the quantity of fiat money at a much faster rate than does the U.S. These disparities in money growth rates are reflected in differences in the growth rates of prices.

The result is not surprising. As illustrated in FIGURE 3.6(b), the fixed price of

FIGURE 3.6

Market for U.S. Dollars

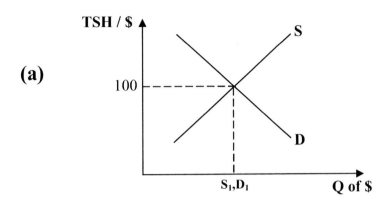

(a)

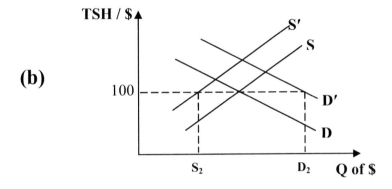

(b)

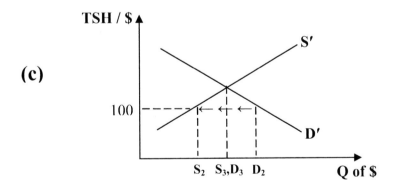

(c)

100 TSH = \$1 no longer is a market clearing one. Because prices in Tanzania increased more rapidly than they did in the U.S., Tanzanian goods have lost price-competitiveness. As a consequence, the demand curve for dollars shifts to the right (from D to D') and the supply curve shifts to the left (from S to S'). The Tanzanian shilling now is overvalued relative to how the market would price the currency. The result is an excess demand for dollars in the market ($D_2 - S_2$), i.e., Tanzania is experiencing balance of payments difficulties.

There are consequences if a country such as Tanzania maintains an inflationary monetary policy but resists devaluation. First, the central bank draws down its holdings of foreign exchange reserves to finance the deficits. In the limit, these reserves approach zero. Second, the ability of a country to borrow additional reserves from international lending agencies (such as the IMF) diminishes. Once such agencies become concerned about the country's ability to repay its debts, they may refuse to lend additional reserves. With a continuing shortage of foreign exchange, the central bank has but two choices. It can acquiesce to market forces and adjust the exchange rate downward. Alternatively, it can attempt to circumvent the market by restricting capital (or money) flows.

How governments in this situation respond depends on whether they are committed to preserving (or increasing) trade flows. When the major trading countries fixed foreign exchange prices under the adjustable peg-system, they usually gave high priority to accommodating demand for foreign exchange and increasing world trade. Many governments in LDCs have not. When confronted with the choice of adjusting exchange rates or restricting capital flows, many have opted for "managed trade." In foreign exchange markets, managed trade means that central banks limit access to foreign exchange rather than accommodate the demand for foreign exchange.

In FIGURE 3.6(c), the Bank of Tanzania attempts to suppress the level of demand for foreign exchange along the path indicated by the arrows. The objective is to force quantity demanded to the level of available supply (S_2). If successful, trade flows are reduced because the quantity of foreign exchange traded (S_2) is below levels traded when central banks accommodate demand (D_2) or when they devalue to the equilibrium price ($S_3 = D_3$).

A. Consequences of an Overvalued Exchange Rate

Decisions by governments in less developed countries to fix the price of foreign exchange and to maintain an overvalued exchange rate (relative to market valuation) importantly influences the structure of foreign exchange markets. Such policies invariably lead to the implementation of exchange controls. In addition, they limit the medium of exchange function of money if the currencies of these countries become nonconvertible. Finally, their policies often encourage black markets in foreign exchange.

i) Exchange Controls

Exchange controls are government laws that attempt to strictly regulate the form of foreign exchange transactions. Although there is some variation from country-to-country, they generally take the following form. All economic agents (domestic and foreign) engaging in foreign exchange transactions are restricted to making exchanges with the government. Those selling foreign exchange must sell to the government. Likewise, buyers are only permitted to purchase from the government. Normally, government participation is through the central bank or an agent of the bank (e.g., a designated commercial bank).

The function of exchange controls is to allocate foreign exchange when price is not permitted to assume this role. In FIGURE 3.6(c), for example, the dollar is undervalued relative to how the market would price it. At the government-determined price, there is excess demand for dollars. With exchange controls, economic agents must not only have the willingness to purchase foreign exchange, but governmental approval as well. Government intent is to suppress effective demand (along the path of arrows) to the level of the available supply. This is accomplished by denying requests for foreign exchange in the amount of $D_2 - S_2$.

When administratively allocating foreign exchange, governments typically apply the following guidelines. Foreign exchange will be allocated to those who propose to use it for "essential" purposes, but will be denied those who propose to use it for other ("nonessential") purposes. An essential purpose generally is one that is consistent with broad policy goals decreed by the government. Examples of such goals are economic growth, capital formation, and increased agricultural output. Nonessential purposes are those not consistent with such policy goals. Requests for foreign exchange to purchase consumer "luxury" goods are an example.

Because government pricing and allocation of foreign exchange politicizes the market, equity issues soon arise. Individuals may fail to acquire foreign exchange, not because they are unwilling to pay the price, but because some government official decided that they would not receive the foreign exchange. Moreover, those administering the allocation process often have a broader interpretation of who qualifies as an "essential" user of foreign exchange. It can include (among others) brothers-in-law, other family members, members of the same tribe, or old secondary school cronies. Such behavior further aggravates equity concerns about the allocation of foreign exchange.

In addition to politicizing foreign exchange markets, exchange controls impose heavy costs on a country's citizens. A major cost is a significant reduction in economic freedom. Exchange controls restrict whom individuals trade with, the number and quality of goods and services available for them to purchase, and where they are allowed to travel. Travel restrictions occur because foreign travel normally is classified as a "nonessential" use of foreign exchange. Especially heavy bearers of these costs are the relatively poor, who often lack the necessary political connections to gain access to foreign exchange.

Exchange controls also lower living standards. They reduce the gains from trade that result from voluntary exchange. Individuals must substitute less preferred for more preferred choices. For some, it might mean purchasing an additional item of clothing instead of the more preferred visit to relatives in a neighboring country. Others may have to forego employment opportunities that are no longer possible. In each of these cases, the result is the same: a reduction in economic welfare.

ii) Non-convertible Currencies

A convertible currency is one that can be converted readily into another currency of one's choice. For this reason, convertible currencies are accepted by market

121

participants as international exchange media. Nearly all international trade is conducted with these monies, with the U.S. dollar the most popular. Nonconvertible currencies, by contrast, can not be converted readily into another currency of one's choice. Consequently, they generally are not accepted as payment in international transactions.

To better understand the distinction between convertible and nonconvertible currencies, consider the series of transactions which are summarized in EXHIBITS 3.6 and 3.7. Each transaction is numbered. They involve an overseas purchase and the tracing of the monetary claim used to finance the purchase.

Individual A in country A purchases goods (G) from Firm B in country B. Payment is made by a check (Chk$_A$) drawn on Bank A, which also is in country A. The transaction is recorded as 1) in the balance sheet of both participants (EXHIBIT 3.6). Individual A shows an increase in its inventory of goods on the asset side of its balance sheet. The check used to make the purchase (Chk$_A$) is the offsetting liability. Firm B swaps assets. It now owns a check (denominated in foreign money) which it acquired by drawing down its inventory of goods.

Firm B is interested in domestic money --- not the foreign money it received in exchange. Thus, it sends the check to its commercial bank (Bank B1), and receives demand deposits (denominated in domestic money) in exchange. This transaction is recorded in the balance sheet of both participants as 2). Bank B1 holds the check, which it acquired by increasing the deposit balance of firm B. Bank B1 now sends the check to the central bank and receives deposit credit for it, i.e., its deposit balance (MBD) at the central bank increased in the amount of the check. Central Bank B now owns the foreign monetary claim (CHK$_A$). The deposit balance of Bank B1 is the offsetting entry. These

EXHIBIT 3.6

T-Accounts for an International Transaction

Individual A

1) Goods +	1) Chk_A +
---	---
6) DD –	6) Chk_A –

Firm B

1) Goods –	
1) Chk_A +	
---	---
2) Chk_A –	
2) DD +	

Bank A

5) Chk_A +	
5) MBD –	
---	---
6) Chk_A –	6) DD –

Bank B1

2) Chk_A +	2) DD +
---	---
3) Chk_A –	
3) MBD +	

Central Bank A

4) Chk_A +	4) Chk_{B2} +
---	---
5) Chk_A –	5) MBD –
---	---
8) DD_F –	8) Chk_{B2} –

Central Bank B

3) Chk_A +	3) MBD +
---	---
4) Chk_A –	
4) Chk_{B2} +	
---	---
7) Chk_{B2} –	7) MBD –

Bank B2

7) Chk_{B2} +	
7) MBD –	
---	---
8) Chk_{B2} –	8) DD_F –

transactions are recorded as 3) in the balance sheets of the participants.

Because the check is a foreign monetary claim, the central bank in country B has several options. It could deposit the check in a bank in country A, and increase its holdings of foreign exchange reserves. Instead, Central Bank B presents the monetary claim to the central bank in country A (Central Bank A). It requests a monetary claim denominated in its own money, and receives a check drawn by Central Bank A on Bank B2 in country B. Note that this decision by Central Bank B will have the effect of reducing the foreign exchange reserves of Central Bank A. This transaction involving the two central banks, is recorded as 4). Each bank gives up a check denominated in the currency of the other country in exchange for one denominated in its own currency.

Both central banks proceed to clear the checks. In country A, Central Bank A sends the check it received to the bank upon which it is drawn (Bank A). Because it is giving up an instrument of value, it reduces the deposit balance of Bank A at the central bank by the same amount. Bank A now holds Chk_A that it obtained by reducing its cash balance at Central Bank A. The entries associated with this transaction are entered as 5). In transaction 6), Bank A cancels the check, and reduces the deposit balance of Individual A. The check originally issued to finance the imported goods now has cleared the banking system.

In country B, Central Bank B sends Chk_{B2} to the bank upon which it is drawn (Bank B2), and reduces the balance of that bank at the Central Bank (MBD) by the same amount---transaction (7). As the final transaction (8), Bank B2 cancels the check and reduces the deposit balance (DD_f) of the drawer. The drawer, in this case, is Central Bank A. Because this deposit balance was a portion of Central Bank A's foreign exchange holdings, country A's foreign exchange reserves are now lower. The origin of this loss of reserves was the importation of goods by individual A. For a summary of net balance sheet changes for all participants, refer to EXHIBIT 3.7 below.

In this example, the currency of country A is a convertible currency. The critical transaction in this sequence is 4). With that exchange of checks, Central Bank A repatriated a monetary instrument from Country A that had been sent overseas to finance a purchase. So long as Central Bank A continues this practice, the country will have a convertible currency. Overseas traders accepting Country A's money will have no difficulty exchanging it for their currency of choice.

If, on the other hand, Central Bank A refuses Central Bank B's request to

---

EXHIBIT 3.7

Net Changes in Balance Sheets

Country A		**Country B**	

Private Nonbank Sector

Goods	+		
DD	-		

Private Nonbank Sector

Goods	-		
DD	+		

Bank Sector

MBD	-	DD	-

Bank Sector

		DD	+
		DD_F	-

Central Bank A

DD_F	-	MBD	-

Central Bank B

125

exchange monies, Central Bank B is left holding a foreign monetary instrument (from Country A) that it is unable to convert into its own money. Once this happens, Central Bank B will no longer accept bank drafts drawn upon banks in Country A. Commercial banks and other economic agents in country B (and other countries), likewise, will refuse such drafts. At this point, Country A's money ceases to be an international medium of exchange. In other words, it is a nonconvertible currency,

The government of a country determines whether its currency is convertible or nonconvertible. Countries with nonconvertible currencies have them because their governments chose to have nonconvertible currencies. This decision most often is not made directly, but is a by-product of other decisions. The first is the decision by a government to fix the price of its currency in foreign exchange markets. This, by itself, is not sufficient for a country to have a nonconvertible currency. What normally is required, as well, is a monetary policy that results in inflation rates appreciably higher than those of competitors. Countries with conservative monetary policies can blend government price-fixing in foreign exchange markets with convertible currencies. The major trading countries did so under the (IMF's) adjustable-peg system.

Many less developed countries, however, have combined rapid monetary growth with fixed exchange rates established by government. The consequences are quite predictable. These countries run balance of payments deficits. By accommodating the excess demand for foreign exchange, they exhaust their holdings of foreign exchange reserves. When these reserves approach zero in the limit, a country has three choices.[32] First, it can choose to let the market determine the price of its currency. Second, it can

---

[32] It is assumed here that the country also has exhausted its potential for borrowing foreign exchange.

adopt a more restrictive monetary policy. Or, third, it can move to a nonconvertible

currency. Countries with nonconvertible currencies have selected the last option.

The decision by a government to have a nonconvertible currency has important

monetary implications for its citizens. They now face a dual monetary economy. While

it is possible for them to use money issued by their government to make domestic

purchases, they cannot use that money when making foreign purchases. The latter

require payment in convertible currencies that other countries issue.[33]

A more important monetary implication of the use of nonconvertible currencies is

that they reinforce the effectiveness of exchange controls. If a country has exchange

controls but a convertible currency, economic agents can attempt to circumvent controls

by using domestic money to pay for foreign goods. With a nonconvertible currency,

however, that option is not available. One must pay with foreign money, and compliance

with foreign exchange control laws means obtaining that money from the government.

Obtaining foreign money, however, may not be possible where governments routinely

deny access to foreign exchange.

iii) Black Markets

Government price-fixing in foreign exchange markets is a necessary condition for

the existence of black markets. Remove the price-fixing and there is no black market.

The reason is simple. If traders are free to establish the price, they will do so at a level

that will clear the market. In FIGURE 3.7, this occurs at the price of 300 Tanzanian

---

[33] When the money issued by foreign governments also is used to make domestic purchases, it is referred to as currency substitution. This has become more prevalent in less developed countries with rapid money growth and a commensurate decline in the purchasing power of their money. Currency substitution is simply a generalization of monetary behavior occurring when countries adopt nonconvertible currencies.

shillings per dollar. At this price, all those willing to buy and sell are able to do so. Thus, there is no economic incentive to devote resources to the activity of reallocating available foreign exchange.

Government price-fixing is not a sufficient condition for the existence of black markets in foreign exchange. There are two situations where it does not lead to black market activity. The first occurs when the government fixes the price at the market-

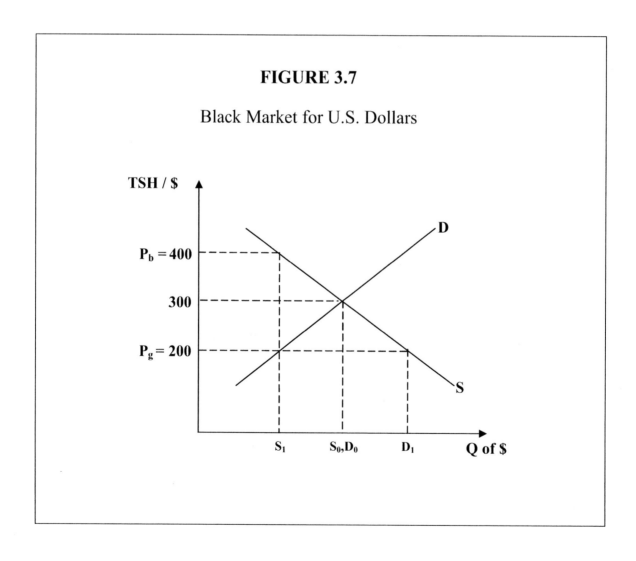

FIGURE 3.7

Black Market for U.S. Dollars

clearing price. If, in the market depicted in FIGURE 3.7, the government of Tanzania selects a price of 300 shillings per dollar, all buyers and sellers are accommodated. Hence, there is no economic basis for any black market activity.

If the government fixes the price of foreign exchange at a level which is not a market-clearing one, there need not be black market activity if the government assumes the role of buffer in the market. In this case, the government must be willing and able to accommodate traders by supplying foreign exchange in situations of excess demand, and purchasing foreign exchange when there is excess supply. In FIGURE 3.7, for example, at the government-determined price (P_g) of 200 shillings per dollar, the government must draw down its foreign exchange reserves in the amount of $D_1 - S_1$. By supplying this amount of foreign exchange to the market, all those demanding foreign exchange are accommodated.

Black markets thrive where government price-fixing results in excess demand for foreign exchange, but the government does not (or can not) play the role of market buffer. If, at the price of 200 shillings per dollar, the government does not supply foreign exchange to the market, not all traders willing to purchase dollars are able to do so. These excess demand pressures persist even when the government successfully suppresses effective demand through the use of exchange controls and nonconvertible currencies. That is, there are still numerous traders who are willing to buy dollars at the prevailing price but are unable to do so because they lack government approval. It is these individuals who are rationed out of the market by exchange controls, and they are the ones black market traders are attempting to accommodate.

Not only are there dissatisfied buyers in the market, but sellers, too, have reason to be disgruntled. Note that in FIGURE 3.7, the quantity of dollars S_1 would be demanded at a price of 400 shillings. If everyone complies with foreign exchange laws, sellers receive 200 shillings per dollar less than market participants would be willing to pay. Another way of looking at this situation is that sellers are required to pay a tax of 200 shillings per dollar in order to exchange dollars for shillings. This is equivalent to a 50 percent tax rate. More generally, the tax rate (t) is: $t = 1 - (P_g/P_b)$, where Pg is the government price for foreign exchange, and P_b is the black market price.

The existence of unsatisfied customers provides a market for the services of black market traders. What are these traders able to deliver to customers? Sellers receive a higher price for the foreign exchange that they sell. Buyers benefit, too, because the supply of foreign exchange potentially is greater and the source more dependable.

In FIGURE 3.7, if all sellers of dollars do so in the black market, the extra proceeds available are equal to 200 shillings per dollar times the quantity of dollars sold: $[(P_b - P_g)(S_1)]$. The reward for selling in the black market, which can be substantial, varies directly with the spread between the black market price and the government decreed price. In this case, sellers obtain two times as many shillings per dollar as they would had they sold to the government.

With black market activity, it is possible that the quantity of foreign exchange available may exceed S_1. Higher prices available in the black market provide an incentive to increase the total supply of foreign exchange. If this happens, the result is a movement up the supply curve in FIGURE 3.7. With greater availability, more buyers of foreign exchange are accommodated. Moreover, excess demand pressures are reduced.

Aside from potentially boosting supply, black markets often offer buyers a more dependable source of supply. Given an excess demand for foreign exchange, buyers relying on government as their source of supply do not always obtain needed foreign exchange. This creates difficulties because many businesses are predicated on a continuous supply of foreign exchange. Some need imported machinery or spare parts in order to operate. Others rely on imported goods for redistribution at the retail level. Because their livelihood depends on satisfying customers, the black market provides an attractive option. Purchasers willing to pay the black market price generally are able to secure a steady source of supply.

The allocative role played by black markets is illustrated in FIGURE 3.7. Assume that black market activity does not increase the supply of foreign exchange, and that all available dollars (S_1) are sold at the black market price of 400 shillings. Market disequilibrium, due to government price-fixing, is eliminated through the process of price rationing. Available supply is distributed to relatively high value users. All buyers willing to pay the black market price (P_b) obtain access to foreign exchange that often was unavailable when they attempted to purchase from the government.

Governments respond unfavorably to black market activities, and understandably so. For, their net effect is to reallocate foreign exchange away from the government and to the private sector. Hence, it is not uncommon for governmental officials to use terminology such as "corrupt, greedy, and profiteers" to describe the activity of these black market traders. In defense of the traders, it is important to remember the source of the area $[(P_b-P_g)(S_1)]$ in FIGURE 3.7. It does not exist because of black market activity. Rather, it is the result of price distortions brought about by government price-fixing.

If all S_1 dollars are sold to the government at the official price of 200 shillings, and none are sold in the black market, the problem of price distortion still exists. The government now has the same problem that originally confronted suppliers of dollars to the market. It acquired dollars at a price of 200 shillings, but the market value of those dollars is 400 shillings.

The government has two options. First, it can sell all S_1 dollars at the official price of 200 shillings. (After all, this is the official price!) Those buying from the government at this price are, indeed, very fortunate individuals. They are paying only one-half of the market value for the dollars they acquire. If they use these dollars to buy imported goods, the government is, in effect, subsidizing those purchases. If they choose not to buy imports, the minute they walk out of the bank they are able to sell their newly acquired dollars (in the black market) for two times their purchase price. In either case, it's a gift.

A second possibility is that government officials allocating the dollars accept bribes for these dollars. There are not enough dollars to satisfy existing demand at the official price, and buyers are willing to pay more. Given current demand, all S_1 dollars could be sold at a price of 400 shillings. In other words, the area $[(P_b-P_g)(S_1)]$ originally available to those supplying dollars to the market is still there for government officials to exploit. If government officials sell all S_1 dollars for 400 shillings per dollar, and record those transactions at the official price of 200 shillings, the area $[(P_b-P_g)(S_1)]$ now represents total bribery income accruing to those officials.

As noted above, exchange controls and nonconvertible currencies impose costs by reducing economic freedom and living standards. While black market traders provide valuable services to buyers and sellers of foreign exchange, their services are not without

cost. Resources employed in these activities could have been used in alternative

productive endeavors. The loss of this potential output represents yet a further reduction

in living standards as a consequence of the government decision to fix the price of

foreign exchange.

VI. Fiat Money and Flexible Exchange Rates

Flexible exchange rates are an alternative to a fixed exchange rate system. In this

case, market traders buy and sell foreign exchange at any price they find mutually

agreeable. From an historical perspective, the world has limited experience with flexible

exchange rates. Most countries with relatively high living standards, however, have

employed them for the more than three decades. It was less common to observe less

developed countries with flexible exchange rates, but their numbers have increased

markedly following the collapse of socialist economies in the 1990s.

A. Short-Run Exchange Rate Determination

Analysis of price determination in markets with flexible exchange rates differs

little from the analysis of other flexible-price markets. Underlying conditions of supply

and demand determine market price. When these conditions change, so does market

price. Factors affecting quantities of foreign exchange demanded and supplied appear as

independent (or right-hand side) variables in demand and supply functions 3.2) and 3.3)

respectively.

3.2) $D = f(ER, P_d, P_f, i_d, i_f, v)$

3.3) $S = f(ER, P_d, P_f, i_d, i_f, u)$

> where, D and S are quantity demanded and
> supplied respectively,
> ER is the foreign exchange rate (the number of units of
> domestic money per unit of foreign money),
> P_d is the domestic price level,
> P_f is the foreign price level,
> i_d is the domestic interest rate,
> i_f is the foreign interest rate,
> v is a variable capturing all other
> factors affecting the quantity demanded,
> and, u is a variable capturing all other
> factors affecting the quantity supplied.

The quantity demanded of foreign exchange depends on a number of factors. Quantity demanded (D) and the exchange rate (ER), for example, are inversely related. As the exchange rate declines, foreign goods become less expensive and the quantity demanded of foreign exchange increases. Changes in the prices of goods and services, likewise, affect the demand for exchange. An increase in domestic prices (P_d), other things equal, increases the demand for foreign goods and, hence, the demand for foreign exchange. In this case, the relationship between D and P_d is direct. For foreign prices (p_f), however, the relationship is indirect. Higher foreign prices make domestic goods more attractive, and reduce the demand for foreign exchange.

Higher domestic interest rates (i_d) reduce the demand for foreign exchange; higher foreign interest rates (i_f) increase the demand. These relationships result from the sensitivity of savers to relative rates of return on financial instruments. The higher the return on domestic securities (i_d), other things equal, the lower the demand for foreign exchange to purchase foreign financial instruments. On the other hand, a higher return on foreign securities (i_f), with the return on domestic securities held constant, increases the demand for foreign securities. Increased demand for foreign securities implies a greater demand for foreign exchange.

Demand function 3.2) is a multi-dimensional relationship. For graphical expositions, the two-dimensional demand schedule is preferred. It is a locus of points showing the quantity of foreign exchange demanded at each exchange rate, *ceteris paribus*. The demand schedule is derived from a demand function in the following manner. Hold all independent variables other than the exchange rate constant. Vary the exchange rate, and trace out the relationship between the quantity demanded and the exchange rate.

The supply side of the market is developed analogously. Those supplying foreign exchange are demanding domestic money. They are doing so in order to purchase domestic goods and services and financial instruments. The quantity of foreign exchange supplied (S) is positively related to the exchange rate. A higher exchange rate, other things equal, means that prices of domestic goods are less expensive to foreigners. As they respond by purchasing more domestically produced goods, the quantity supplied of foreign exchange increases. Changes in relative price levels, likewise, affect the supply of foreign exchange. As domestic prices increase, with foreign prices held constant, domestic goods become less price-competitive, and the supply of foreign exchange falls. The opposite, an increase in the supply of foreign exchange, occurs when foreign prices increase relative to domestic prices.

Relative interest rates also affect supply of foreign exchange. Higher domestic interest rates increase the supply of foreign exchange because foreigners now find domestic financial instruments more attractive. Higher foreign interest rates, on the other hand, reduce the supply of foreign exchange. In this case, more foreigners opt for securities issued in their own countries at the expense of securities issued elsewhere.

Following the approach used when analyzing demand, a *ceteris paribus* assumption is employed to derive the supply schedule (or curve) from the supply function. One must hold the values of all independent variables other than the exchange rate constant. Tracing out the resulting locus of points representing the quantity of foreign exchange supplied at each exchange rate yields the supply schedule.

Price determination in the market involves the interaction of supply and demand forces. These forces are depicted graphically as demand and supply schedules in FIGURE 3.8. Equilibrium price, or the market clearing exchange rate, is ER_0. At this price, the quantity of foreign exchange willingly supplied (S_0) is exactly equal to the quantity willingly demanded (D_0).

At any other price, the market is in disequilibrium. At exchange rate ER_1, there is excess demand ($D_1 - S_1$) for foreign exchange. Not all buyers are able to obtain foreign exchange at this price, and competition among them forces the exchange rate upward. The opposite adjustment occurs at price ER_2. Here, there is excess supply of foreign exchange ($S_2 - D_2$) and competition among sellers forces the price downward. By adjusting to clear the market, exchange rates play a critical rationing role in foreign exchange markets.

The gravitation of market price towards its equilibrium level does not imply a stationary foreign exchange rate. In open markets, exchange rates change continuously because underlying market conditions are subject to continuous variation. With varying

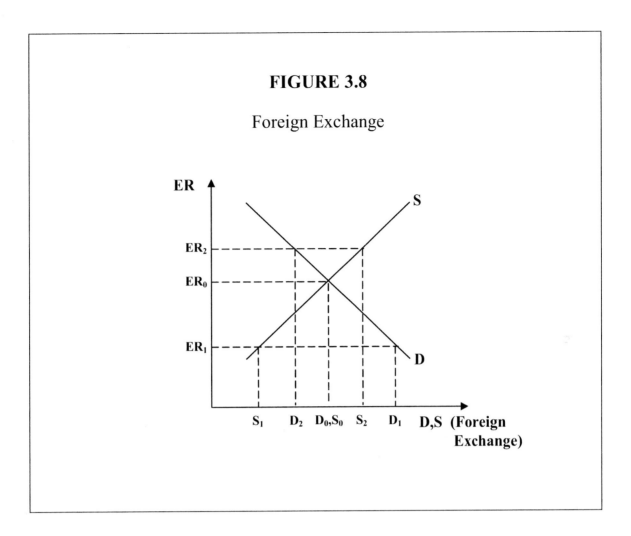

FIGURE 3.8

Foreign Exchange

market conditions, price changes are necessary if the market is to coordinate the diverse plans of multitudes of traders.

From an analytical standpoint, changes in market conditions are captured by relaxing the *ceteris paribus* assumption. This occurs with any change in a variable other than the exchange rate (ER) in equation 3.2) or 3.3). If a variable in the demand function changes, the result is a shift in the demand schedule. For a change in a variable in the supply function, it is the supply schedule that shifts. Both schedules shift when a variable changes that appears in both functions. To facilitate understanding, it is customary to change one independent variable at a time and to examine the implications of that change. That procedure is adopted here.

Domestic prices (P_d) are positively related to the demand for foreign exchange (equation 3.2) and negatively to the supply (equation 3.3). Hence, an increase in the domestic price level causes the demand curve to shift to the right and the supply schedule to shift to the left. At the previously prevailing exchange rate (ER_0), there now is excess demand for foreign exchange. Competition among purchasers forces the price of foreign exchange higher, i.e., foreign money appreciates in value relative to domestic money. This situation is shown in FIGURE 3.9a, where the new equilibrium price is ER_1. Had the domestic price level fallen, instead, domestic goods would become more competitive in international markets. Domestic money would have appreciated in value on the foreign exchange market.

Changes in foreign prices (P_f) also affect relative prices and the exchange rate. The demand for foreign exchange is negatively related to the foreign price level; the supply of foreign exchange, positively related. An increase in foreign prices (other things equal) causes the demand curve for foreign exchange to shift to the left and the supply curve to shift to the right (FIGURE 3.9b). As a consequence, the equilibrium exchange rate falls from ER_0 to ER_1. Domestic money appreciates in value in the foreign exchange market or, equivalently, foreign exchange depreciates in value. The opposite occurs when foreign prices fall.

Changing capital flows, likewise, affect exchange rates. Movements in relative interest rate levels are hypothesized to induce such changes. A fall in the domestic interest rate (other things equal), for example, makes domestic securities less competitive

FIGURE 3.9

Foreign Exchange Market
With Parametric Changes

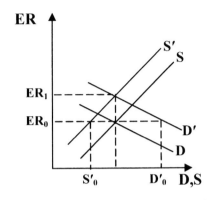

a) increase in domestic price level

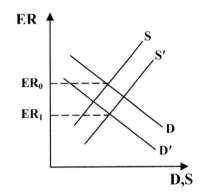

b) increase in foreign price level

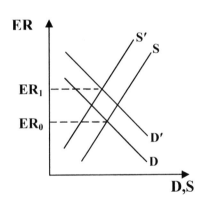

c) decrease in domestic interest rates

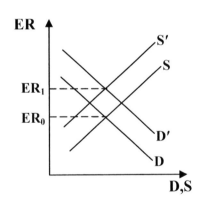

d) increase in foreign interest rates

in global financial markets. Although their level remains unchanged, foreign interest

rates now are more attractive. The result is an increased demand for foreign exchange, a reduced supply, and a higher foreign exchange rate (FIGURE 3.9c). These observed shifts in demand and supply curves are consistent with equations 3.2) and 3.3), where the demand for foreign exchange is inversely related to domestic interest rates and the supply is directly related.

Movements in foreign interest rates affect exchange rates for the same reason, i.e., investors are sensitive to relative rates of return. The quantity of foreign exchange demanded is directly related to foreign interest rates; the quantity supplied, inversely related. A rise in foreign interest rates increases the relative attractiveness of foreign securities. The demand curve for foreign exchange shifts to the right and the supply curve to the left (FIGURE 3.9d). Foreign exchange appreciates in value (or domestic money falls in value). Falling foreign interest rates have the opposite effect.

In summary, when markets are open and traders are free to establish mutually agreeable prices, prices tend to vary continuously because underlying market conditions constantly change. Open markets in foreign exchange conform to this pattern, i.e., exchange rates exhibit continual variation. Two important factors responsible for short-run variation in exchange rates are movements in relative prices and interest rates.

B. The "Dirty Float"

In countries where exchange rates are free to vary, it is not always true that market forces, alone, determine exchange rates. Occasionally, central banks enter foreign exchange markets and buy and sell currencies in order to affect market price. This is referred to as central bank intervention in foreign exchange markets. When it occurs, observed exchange rates are not strictly the result of market forces, but reflect these activities as well. The term "dirty float" is an acknowledgement that central banks do, at times, play this role.

When central banks intervene in foreign exchange markets, they can do so individually or collectively. Recently, collective intervention has been popular. A group of industrial countries known as the G7 are loosely organized for that purpose.[34] Those countries normally justify their collective action as an effort to coordinate macroeconomic policies across countries. Hence, their joint actions frequently are called "policy coordination."

It is doubtful, however, that G7 countries have either the ability or willingness to successfully coordinate macroeconomic policies. To date, such efforts mainly have taken the form of a joint purchases or sales of U.S. dollars---the principal international medium of exchange. The objective has been to bring about a foreign-exchange market price for the U.S. dollar that is different from how market traders would value the dollar.

When the dollar is falling, for example, central banks may agree to purchase dollars in order to keep it from falling further. An intervention of this type is illustrated in FIGURE 3.10, which shows the market for U.S. dollars in terms of Japanese Yen (¥). At the current rate of exchange, $(¥/\$)_0$, there is an excess supply of dollars in the market. If market forces are allowed to operate, the price of the dollar will depreciate to the level

---

[34] Originally, the group consisted of five members known as the "Group of Five" (G5). They were the U.S., the U.K., Japan, France, and Germany. Later, Canada and Italy joined and the G5 became the G7. Russia sometimes attends the meetings.

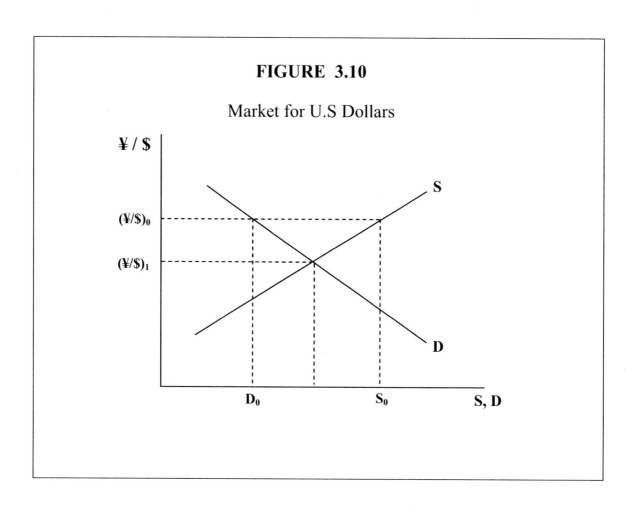

FIGURE 3.10

Market for U.S Dollars

$(¥/\$)_1$. To keep this from happening, central banks must intervene by purchasing dollars in the amount of $(S_0 - D_0)$. These purchases increase the demand for dollars, and the quantity demanded is now exactly equal to the supplied (S_0). Intervention, in this case, keeps the dollar from falling.

The effects of these transactions on the balance sheets of participants are shown in EXHIBIT 3.8. For simplicity purposes, only balance sheets for the intervening central bank (the U.S. Federal Reserve Bank) and a single trader (foreign exchange dealer) are shown. The Federal Reserve's balance sheet shows an increase in the holdings of dollar

EXHIBIT 3.8

Balance Sheet Changes with Intervention

Federal Reserve Bank		Foreign Exchange Dealer	
¥	−	¥	+
$	+	$	−

balances that it acquired by selling Yen. This represents a loss in foreign exchange

reserves for the U.S. central bank. The private trader (Foreign Exchange Dealer), on the

other hand, shows an increase in holdings of ¥ obtained by selling dollars to the Federal

Reserve Bank.

While central banks can temporarily affect the exchange rate, it is much more

difficult in the long-run. This is not surprising because such interventions are an attempt

to override market outcomes.[35] Unless market conditions change, short-term

interventions only delay the movement of an exchange rate. If market conditions do

change, they may well change in a manner that pushes the exchange rate in a direction

opposite to that preferred by the central banks. More intervention now is required and

---

[35] The central banks in question are "swimming against the current." Their interventions are an attempt to keep market price from moving in the direction it is heading.

further erosion of central bank reserves occurs. The continuing loss of foreign exchange reserves is a major factor militating against longer-term intervention by central banks.[36]

Policy ineffectiveness does not imply that central bank interventions are without effect. By diverting focus away from economic considerations, they politicize activity in foreign exchange markets. Pressure groups representing special interests now know where to go if market price moves unfavorably for them. In addition, central bank interventions often result in a transfer of wealth from central banks to private traders. This occurs, for example, when the exchange rate in FIGURE 3.10 eventually falls to its equilibrium level (¥/$)$_1$. As seen in EXHIBIT 3.8, the wealth position of the Federal Reserve Bank has deteriorated because it accumulated assets that fell in value ($U.S.) and disposed of assets that subsequently appreciated in value (¥). Private traders are the beneficiaries. They accumulated Yen-denominated assets that gained value and disposed of U.S. dollar-denominated assets that subsequently depreciated.

C. Long-Run Exchange Rate Determination: Purchasing Power Parity

The law of one price is the proposition that an identical commodity should sell for the same price without regard to its location.[37] Market activity insures this outcome because profit opportunities exist whenever the same commodity sells for two different prices. Traders obtain profit by purchasing in the relatively low-price market and selling in the relatively high-price market. Increasing demand in the relatively low-price market

---

[36] The monetary independence of individual countries also is subverted. After all, long-term intervention is simply another name for government price-fixing in foreign exchange markets.

[37] Exceptions to the law of one price can occur. Transportation costs serve as a "natural" barrier, and a price differential reflecting transportation costs can exist without encouraging arbitrage. Government imposed barriers to trade such as tariffs and quotas also can lead to price differences that are not eliminated by arbitrage activity. These are "artificial" barriers.

and increasing supply in the relatively high-price market results in price convergence and, eventually, a uniform market price. This trading activity is called arbitrage; those practicing it, arbitrageurs.

The purchasing power parity theory (PPP) of exchange rates applies the law of one price to money. Money should only have one price, i.e., it should have purchasing power parity (or equality). In this context, money is not used as a unit of account. The reason is that the exchange value (or price) of a unit of money in terms of money is always one. Rather, the price of money refers to how money exchanges relative to all other goods and services. The relationship is inverse, as is indicated in equation 3.4). An increase in the average price of goods and services (P) is the same thing as a reduction in the purchasing power of money (PPM), or its price. Conversely, with a decrease in the average price, a unit of money will purchase more.

3.4) $PPM = 1/P,$

> where PPM is the purchasing power of money, or
> its price, and P is the average price for goods and
> services.

In the international economy, a unit of money has a single price if it purchases an equivalent amount of goods and services in each country. If it does not, money has more than one price, and profit opportunities exist. This stimulates arbitrage activity, which causes exchange rates to move in a manner that brings about purchasing power parity.

Consider the following example involving two countries: Mexico and the U.S. Rather than considering all goods and services, a simplifying assumption is made. There is only one good, shoes, that are identical in both countries. The shoes sell for $50 in the

U.S., and 500 pesos in Mexico. The current exchange rate is one U.S. dollar for 10 Mexican pesos.

At that exchange rate, purchasing power parity exists for both currencies. Individuals in the U.S. can purchase the shoes in their own country for $50. Alternately, they can exchange $50 for 500 pesos in the foreign exchange market, and purchase the same shoes in Mexico for 500 pesos. One U.S. dollar exchanges for 1/50th of a pair of shoes in both countries, i.e., the dollar has purchasing power parity.

For citizens of Mexico, shoes purchased domestically cost 500 pesos. 500 pesos will exchange for $50 in the foreign exchange market, which is exactly the price of that pair of shoes in the U.S. One Mexican peso exchanges for 1/500th of a pair of shoes in both countries, and the Mexican peso also has purchasing power parity.

Now, assume that these two countries follow radically different monetary policies. In the U.S., the money supply does not change, while the Bank of Mexico increases the money supply in that country at the rate of 50 percent per annum. Further, assume that prices (including the price of shoes) mirror money growth in the two countries. That is, the average price of goods and services remains the same in the U.S., but increases at the annual rate of 50 percent in Mexico. After one year, the price of shoes remains at $50 in the U.S., but increases to 750 pesos in Mexico.

At the previously-prevailing exchange rate, neither currency now has purchasing power parity. One U.S. dollar exchanges for 1/50th of a pair of shoes in the U.S., but only 1/75th of a pair of shoes in Mexico. Likewise, one peso now exchanges for 1/750th of a pair of shoes in Mexico, but 1/500th of a pair of shoes in the U.S.

This departure from purchasing power parity gives rise to arbitrage activity in money. The arbitrageurs, in this case, are consumers. Both currencies have a higher price, or exchange value, in the U.S. That is, each will purchase a larger quantity of goods in that country. With consumers in both countries preferring to purchase goods the in U.S., Mexico now experiences a balance of payments deficit (and the U.S., a surplus).

With flexible exchange rates, the value of the Mexican peso will fall (in relation to the dollar) on the foreign exchange market. That is, the peso depreciates in value; the dollar appreciates. Exchange rate adjustment continues until the foreign exchange market clears.

In this example, market clearing occurs at the exchange rate: 15 p = \$1. At this exchange rate, both monies again have purchasing power parity. The dollar purchases $1/50^{th}$ of a pair of shoes both in the U.S. and in Mexico. The Mexican peso will purchase $1/750^{th}$ of a pair in each country. There is no source for further disturbance in the exchange rate.

The adjustment process just described is the purchasing power theory of exchange rates. According to the theory, long-run changes in exchange rates occur primarily because of differences in price-level changes for individual countries. Differences in price-level changes result in a deviation from purchasing power parity. Restoration of purchasing power parity occurs through arbitrage activity in money (and, thus, goods). Money moves from markets where its value is relatively low, to markets where it has a relatively high value. Exchange rates adjust until the monies involved have purchasing power parity, and the law of one price again applies to money.

The purchasing power parity theory has important implications in a world of fiat money. Individual countries have monetary autonomy, i.e., they have the freedom to increase (or decrease) the money supply at their own discretion. Under this monetary arrangement, individual countries have increased the money supply at widely varying rates. The result has been great variation in inflation rates from country-to-country.

Foreign exchange markets, through variation in exchange rates, accommodate these differences in monetary policies. Countries with relatively rapid money growth (and inflation) experience depreciation in their exchange rate. Those with more conservative monetary policies (and lower inflation) experience appreciation.

CHAPTER 4

CENTRAL BANKS AND THE MONEY SUPPLY

I. A Model of the Money Supply..150

    A. Base Money...150

    B. Base Money Equation 154
        i) Federal Reserve Float 156
        ii) Treasury Deposits...159

    C. The (Base) Money Multiplier.......................................161
        i)   The Currency Ratio: k.......................................162
        ii) The Reserve Ratio Requirement: r_r 164
        iii) The Excess Reserve Ratio: r_e...........................165
        iv) A Numeric Example 167

II. General Instruments of Monetary Control 167

    A. Open Market Operations 168
        i)   History 168
        ii) The Process 169
        iii) Accounting for Open Market Operations...............170
        iv) Open Market Operations and the Money Supply 172
        v) Transmission of Bank Reserves............................173

    B. Discount Rate/Discount Window 175

    C. Reserve Ratio Requirements...179

III. Closed Market Operations 182

APPENDIX A.   Derivation of the Base Money Equation...........................185

APPENDIX B.   Derivation of the Base Money Multiplier 189

I. A Model of the Money Supply

This money supply model is used to examine factors that determine the total quantity of money. In its basic form, the components are the level of base money (B), the base money multiplier (m), and the quantity of money (M). The model is presented in the form of both levels and differences (absolute changes).

4.1) $M = B(m)$

4.2) $dM = dB(m) + B(dm)$

Equation 4.1 states that the level of money (money supply) is equal to the level of base money (monetary base, or high-powered money) times the level of the base money multiplier. Equation 4.2 expresses the same relationship in terms of differences. The change in the money supply (dM) depends on changes in the monetary base (dB) and changes in the money multiplier (dm). The M1 measure of money is used in this chapter, although it is possible to use the same general model for other measures.

A. Base Money

The monetary base is the primary form of money. It varies with the type of money used, and generally serves as the foundation for other elements of the money supply. In the case of commodity money, the levels of M and B are the same. Assume, for example, that gold coins are the only form of money. These gold coins serve as the monetary base. Base money is equal to the total quantity of gold coins (G), which is also the level of the money supply. With B and M the same number (equation 4.3), the money multiplier

assumes the trivial value of one. EXHIBIT 4.1 shows the value of the money multiplier

under different monetary systems.

$$4.3) \quad G = B = M$$

With fiduciary and fiat monies, the size of the money multiplier depends upon

whether banks practice 100% reserve banking or fractional reserve banking. 100%

reserve banking is when the banking institution holds bank reserves in the proportion of

100 percent of its deposit liabilities. (Bank reserves are the cash holdings of a bank.)

With fractional reserve banking, a bank's cash reserves are less than 100 percent of its

---

EXHIBIT 4.1

Values for m Under Different Monetary Systems

Type of Money	m
Commodity Money	1
Fiduciary Money	
100% Reserve Banking	1
Fractional Reserve Banking	> 1
Fiat Money	
100% Reserve Banking	1
Fractional Reserve Banking	> 1

deposit liabilities.

Fiduciary money is a hybrid arrangement. It consists of an underlying commodity money, and fiduciary elements that are convertible into commodity money on demand. Assuming again that the commodity money is in the form of gold coins, the total quantity of these gold coins (G) is the monetary base. There are now alternative uses of the monetary base. A portion is used as circulating money (G_M); the remainder, as bank reserves (G_B). This partition appears in equation 4.4).

The total money supply (equation 4.5) is equal to the quantity of circulating gold coins (G_M) plus the quantity of circulating fiduciary money (FG_M) which is convertible into G_M. Fiduciary money is issued by banking institutions. With 100% reserve banking, $G_B = FG_M$. Consequently, $M = B$, and the size of the money multiplier is one. Banks are warehousing money.

$$4.4) \quad B = G_M + G_B$$

$$4.5) \quad M = G_M + FG_M$$

When banks enter the lending business, they practice fractional reserve banking. They either lend a portion of their reserves directly or, alternatively, make additional loans by issuing new fiduciary money. Bank reserves now equal only a portion of deposit liabilities, i.e., $G_B < FG_M$. FG_M includes both convertible currency and bank deposit money, which is only indirectly convertible. Individuals can convert bank deposits into convertible currency and, then, convert that currency into monetary gold.

The important issue here is that the money multiplier is now greater than one (m > 1). Banks are no longer just storing money, but are affecting the size of the money stock.

As noted in Chapter 1, the adoption of fiat money was not a spontaneous market development. Governments confiscated (through forced exchanges) all monetary gold. In addition, laws were passed making it illegal to use gold as an exchange medium. Hence, both elements on the right-hand side of equations 4.4) and 4.5) were no longer available for monetary use, at least in their previous capacities.

The monetary system was reconstituted. The currency and bank deposits previously used as exchange media were still so employed. With no convertibility option (direct or indirect), however, these monies were now fiat money (FM). This is indicated in equation 4.7). Equation 4.6) is the new monetary base, which now consists of total bank reserves plus currency in circulation outside banks.

4.6) $B = R + C$

4.7) $M = FM = DD\sqrt{} + C,$

> Where R is total bank reserves,
> C is currency in circulation outside banks,
> FM is the total quantity of fiat money, and
> $DD\sqrt{}$ is total checkable deposits.

It is possible to have 100% reserve banking with fiat money. In that case, $R = DD\sqrt{}$. In practice, fiat money invariably is coupled with fractional reserve banking. Consequently, the money multiplier for our current monetary system is greater that one.

B. The Base Money Equation

The base money equation is a relationship showing the total quantity of base money as well as the uses and sources of the base. This equation is an accounting identity, and is derived by combining the balance sheet for the central bank with the Treasury monetary account. In the U.S., the combined balance sheet for all 12 Federal Reserve Banks is used as the central bank balance sheet. EXHIBIT 4.2 shows that balance sheet.

Equation 4.8) is the base money equation for the U.S.[38] Nearly all the entries are from the Federal Reserve balance sheet. $R + C$ shows uses of the monetary base. Base money is either used as bank reserves (R) or circulating currency (C). Total bank reserves (R) are viewed as the Federal Reserve defines them: total commercial bank balances at Federal Reserve Banks (MBD) plus total bank vault cash (BVC). Bank vault cash consists of currency holdings by commercial banks. It is in the form of coins issued by the U.S. Treasury (TC_B) and paper notes issued by Federal Reserve banks (FRN_B).

$$4.8) \quad B \equiv R + C \equiv TS + D + F + FE + G + SDR + TC + OFRA - TCH - TRD - FD$$

Currency in circulation (C) is total currency circulating outside of banks. It consists of Treasury-issued coins owned by the public (TC_p) and Federal Reserve Notes owned by the public (FRN_P). When the public goes to the bank (or a teller machine) and withdraws currency, the level of the monetary base remains unchanged but the uses of the monetary base have changed. C increases and R decreases. R falls because bank vault cash (FRN_B) declines. When the public deposits currency, it, likewise, has no effect on the level of base money. The composition of base money, however, again changes.

---

[38] Derivation of this equation appears in APPENDIX A at the end of this Chapter.

EXHIBIT 4.2

Combined Balance Sheet for Federal Reserve Banks

Assets	Liabilities
(TS) U.S. Treasury Securities	Federal Reserve Notes:
(D) Discounts and Advances	(FRN_P) owned by the public
(CIPC) Cash Items in the	(FRN_T) owned by the Treasury
Process of collection	(FRN_B) owned by commercial banks
(FE) Foreign Exchange	
(GC) Gold Certificates	Deposits:
(SDRC) Special Drawing Right	(MBD) owned by commercial banks
Certificates	(TRD) owned by the Treasury
(TC_{FRB}) Treasury Currency	(FD) owned by Foreign Central Banks
Held by Federal Reserve	and International Institutions
Banks	
(OFRA) Other Assets minus	(DACI) Deferred Availability of Cash Items
Other Liabilities and	
Capital Accounts	

All variables to the right of the identity sign (starting with TS) are sources of the monetary base. They include both factors of increase and factors of decrease. Those with a positive sign (TS,D,F,G,...) are factors of increase. If they increase (decrease), and the offsetting accounting entry in equation 4.8) is B, then the monetary base increases (decreases) on a one-to-one basis. Variables with a negative sign (TCH, TRD, FD) are factors of decrease. If they increase (decrease), and the offsetting accounting entry in the base money equation is B, the monetary base decreases (increases). The relationship is one-to-one, but inverse.

i) Federal Reserve Float (F)

The first three terms on the right-hand side of the base money equation (TS, D, and F) all originate in the Fed's balance sheet, and each is a factor of increase. Collectively (TS + D + F) they are called Federal Reserve Credit. This measures the quantity of base money that exists as a consequence of Federal Reserve actions. Aggregate Treasury security holdings by Reserve Banks (TS) and total commercial bank borrowings at the Federal Reserve discount window (D) result from monetary policy, and are discussed below.

The third, Federal Reserve float (F) is not due to monetary policy, but relates to the Federal Reserve procedures for clearing checks. It is calculated as the net of two items in the Federal Reserve balance sheet. Federal Reserve Float is equal to cash items in the process of collection (CIPC) minus deferred availability of cash items (DACI). That is, F = CIPC - DACI.

CIPC is a Federal Reserve asset, and records the volume of cash items in the form of checks that the Fed owns. Banks sent these checks to the Federal Reserve for clearing purposes. How the Federal Reserve pays for these checks also is recorded in the Fed's balance sheet. A few cash items receive immediate (or same day) credit, and the offsetting entry is a liability item in the Federal Reserve balance sheet: MBD. The bank submitting this cash item is credited with bank reserves in the form of a larger checking account balance at the Federal Reserve Bank.

While all banks eventually receive reserves (MBD) for checks they send to the Fed, they do not receive immediate reserve credit for most cash items. Instead, the Federal Reserve schedules to pay them reserves at a later date. According to the Fed's processing procedures, reserve payment will occur either one day later or two days hence. Timing of the payment is based on a predetermined geographic grid as well as the type of cash item submitted. That scheduled payment is entered in the balance sheet as liability item: deferred availability of cash items (DACI).

Note that the Federal Reserve's procedures for giving reserve credit to banks submitting cash items is not determined by when they collect on these checks. Consequently, their clearing procedures have monetary implications. The Federal Reserve often credits a bank (that sent a cash item) with reserves prior to collecting on the check. When that happens, total reserves in the banking system increase. Federal Reserve float is a measure of the total quantity of reserves in the banking system that entered in this manner. The volume of float varies from day-to-day and is influenced by factors such as weather conditions and the geographic features of market sales. Local purchases are less likely to result in Federal Reserve float than are national or international purchases.

An example of Federal Reserve float is shown in EXHIBIT 4.3. In transaction 1), Bank A sends a check to the Federal Reserve Bank. The offsetting entry in the bank's balance sheet is DACI (+), a scheduled payment of bank reserves by the Fed. In the Fed's balance sheet both CIPC and DACI increase by the same amount. Hence, total Federal Reserve float is unchanged.

Assume that two days pass, and the Federal Reserve credits Bank A with reserves (MBD_A +) even though it has yet to collect on the check. This is transaction 2). If one combines transactions 1) and 2), the Federal Reserve balance sheet shows that CIPC is

```
┌─────────────────────────────────────────────────────────────────┐
│                        EXHIBIT 4.3                                │
│                                                                   │
│                    Federal Reserve Float                          │
│                                                                   │
│         Federal Reserve Bank                    Bank A            │
│        ─────────────────────────          ─────────────────────  │
│      1) CIPC   + │ 1) DACI   +      1) CHK    -  │               │
│                  │                  1) DACI   +  │               │
│      - - - - - - │- - - - - - - - - - - - - - - - - - - - - - -  │
│                  │ 2) DACI   -      2) DACI   -  │               │
│                  │ 2) MBD_A  +      2) MBD_A  +  │               │
│                                                                   │
│                                                                   │
│              dF   =   dCIPC   -   dDACI                            │
│          ─────────────────────────────────                        │
│            1)    0        +          +                            │
│            2)    +        0          -                            │
│          ─────────────────────────────────                        │
└─────────────────────────────────────────────────────────────────┘
```

up, but DACI is not. Federal Reserve float increased with the second transaction.

The Fed will eventually collect on this check and, when they do, they will reduce the reserves of the Bank B (MBD_B -), the bank upon which the check is drawn. This check will have effectively cleared the system, and there is no longer any float associated with that instrument. The increase in reserves at Bank A is exactly offset by a drop in reserves at Bank B.

ii) Treasury Deposits (TRD)

Treasury deposits (TRD) is also a variable in the base money equation. The U.S. Treasury uses Federal Reserve Banks for banking purposes. It owns deposit balances at Reserve banks, and writes checks on those balances in order to make payments. Those deposit balances are referred to as Treasury deposits (TRD), and appear as a liability item on the combined balance sheet for Federal Reserve Banks.

This item in the Fed's balance sheet (TRD) also appears as a factor of decrease in the base money equation (4.8). When the Treasury writes a check on its account, the check ultimately clears the banking system. The commercial bank submitting the check to the Federal Reserve receives deposit credit at a Federal Reserve Bank. Thus, bank reserves (and base money, B) increase, but TRD falls when the Federal Reserve Bank cancels the check the Treasury wrote to make the payment. The opposite happens when someone sends a check to the Treasury and the Treasury deposits that check at a Reserve Bank. TRD increases and MBD decreases.

Consider an example where individual A, who banks at Bank A, makes a tax payment to the Treasury. Payment by individual A is in the form of a check drawn on Bank A. The T-accounts for this transaction are in EXHIBIT 4.4. Only final entries in the T-accounts are shown, i.e., intermediate transactions such as the deposit and the clearing of the check do not appear.

Having written a check to pay his taxes, individual A now has a lower checking account balance (DD√ -). The offsetting balance sheet entry is a decline in his net worth (NW). That occurs because the tax payment is not a *quid pro quo* transaction. The tax payment is compulsory with no specific goods or services received in exchange.

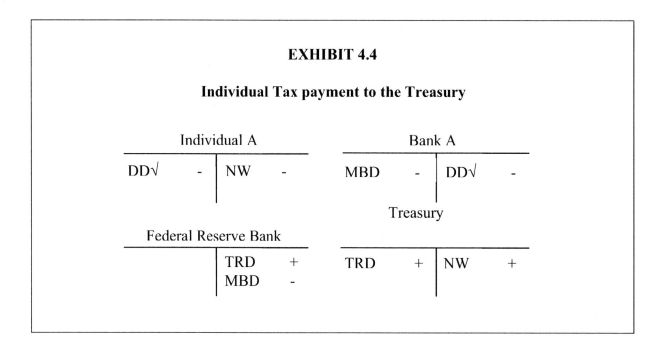

EXHIBIT 4.4

Individual Tax payment to the Treasury

Individual A				Bank A			
DD√	-	NW	-	MBD	-	DD√	-

Treasury

Federal Reserve Bank							
		TRD	+	TRD	+	NW	+
		MBD	-				

The balance sheet for Bank A shows individual A's lower deposit balance. This is offset by Bank A's lower deposit balance at the Federal Reserve Bank (MBD -). The Treasury deposited individual A's check at the Federal Reserve Bank. When the Fed sent that check back to Bank A (for clearing purposes), it lowered Bank A's deposit balance as payment for the check.

The Treasury now has a larger cash balance at the Federal Reserve Bank (TRD +), with the offsetting entry an increase in its new worth (NW +). With its higher cash balances, the Treasury is now in a position to purchase more goods and services. As a consequence of paying taxes, the private sector (individual A) is in a position to purchase fewer.

From a monetary standpoint, base money is lower. That is because TRD is a factor of decrease in the base money equation. The reduction in base money appears in T-accounts as a decline in MBD. These deposits are a component of bank reserves. Thus, in equation 4.8, B (in the form of R) is lower, while TRD is higher.

Treasury management of its cash position, then, affects the quantity of base money. Hence, Treasury actions can potentially impair the effectiveness of monetary policy. For that reason, there is daily communication between the Treasury and the Federal Reserve concerning Treasury budgetary activity for that day. This allows the central bank an opportunity to take actions that offset the monetary repercussions of Treasury fiscal actions.

C. The (Base) Money Multiplier

In a world of fiat money with fractional reserve banking, the money multiplier is greater than one. This means that whenever the level of base money changes, the money supply changes by some multiple of that change in the base. The extent of the change in money supply depends on the size of the base money multipler (m). The M1-multiplier is presented as equation 4.9).[39]

$$4.9) \quad m = (1 + k) / (r_r + r_e + k)$$

> where k is the currency ratio,
> r_r is the reserve ratio requirement, and
> r_e is the excess reserve ratio.

$$4.10) \quad k = C / DD\sqrt{}$$

> where, C is total currency in circulation outside banks, and
> $DD\sqrt{}$ is total checkable deposits.

---

[39] The derivation of the M1-multiplier is found in APPENDIX B at the end of the chapter.

4.11) $r_r = RR / DD\sqrt{}$

where RR is total required reserves for banking institutions.

4.12) $r_e = ER / DD\sqrt{}$

where ER is total excess reserves held by banks.

i) The Currency Ratio: k

There are three factors that determine the size of m: k, r_r, and r_e. The first, k, is the currency ratio (equation 4.10). It is a behavioral ratio, whose value is determined by the general public. The currency ratio measures how much currency the public chooses to hold relative to their holdings of checkable deposits. k is also an aggregate ratio, i.e., the value of k is an average ratio for the entire public.

Because k appears in both the numerator and denominator of the money multiplier, it is not immediately clear whether the relationship between m and k is direct or inverse. If k increases, both the numerator and denominator of m increase. Similarly, a decline in k results in a lower value for both the numerator and denominator.

While the mathematics is not developed here, for reasonable values of the other parameters in m, the relationship between m and k is inverse ($\partial m / \partial k < 0$.) The change in m divided by the change in k is less than zero. Increases in the currency ratio cause the money multiplier to fall; decreases cause it to rise.

The reason for this inverse relationship becomes apparent by examining equations 4.13) and 4.14). It has to do with how the monetary base is used. Every unit of base money that is held as circulating currency (C) maps into exactly one unit of money (M1).

162

The relationship is one-to-one. On the other hand, every unit of base money that is used as bank reserves maps to some multiple of that value in terms of money. The relationship is one-to-x, where x > 1.

4.13) B = R + C

4.14) M1 = DD√ + C

Thus, base money supports a larger money supply when it is used as bank reserves. The reason is fractional reserve banking (R < DD√). When individuals deposit their currency in banks, that currency becomes bank reserves (R ↑ and C ↓). These bank reserves support some multiple level of deposit money in a world of fractional reserve banking. Had the individuals continued using the currency instead of depositing it, there would be no such multiple impact on the money supply.

When the currency ratio (k) changes, so, too, does the money supply. Consequently the portfolio behavior of the general public has monetary significance. Decisions concerning how much currency to hold relative to deposit money influence the money supply through changes in the money multiplier.

There are seasonal, cyclical, and secular influences on the public's portfolio behavior (and, thus, k). An important seasonal influence is the Christmas holiday season in the U.S. Related to the sharp acceleration in December retail sales is a greater demand for currency to effectuate those sales. The higher currency ratio has a depressive influence on the money multiplier and the money stock. That upward blip in the currency-ratio generally is reversed in January, when retail sales most often fall.

One of the more dramatic movements in the currency-ratio occurred during the great depression in the 1930s. The public lost confidence in commercial banks and many chose to hold their money in the form of currency rather than bank deposits. This led to a sharp decline in the money multiplier, which contributed significantly to a massive decline in the money supply.

During the process of economic development the currency ratio tends to fall. This secular decline is related to the development of financial institutions and markets. As these institutions and markets develop, the public usually reduces its reliance on currency, and more frequently makes payment with deposit money. One hundred years ago, for example, it was not uncommon for U.S. workers to receive their wages in the form of currency. That rarely occurs today. Most individuals receive payment either by check or via direct deposit.

ii) The Reserve Ratio Requirement: r_r

Banking is a very highly regulated industry. That is true even in those countries where most markets are open, and voluntary exchange generally is permitted. One form of banking regulation is reserve requirements. This regulation requires banks to hold reserves in a specified minimum ratio to their deposit liabilities.

While it is possible to have reserve requirements for several categories of bank deposits, only the reserve requirement on checkable deposits (r_r) is considered here. If r_r = 10%, for example, banks are required to hold reserves in the proportion of at least 10 percent of their checkable deposit liabilities. Equation 4.15) shows the calculation for required reserves (RR). If r_r = 10%, and total DD√ is equal to one million dollars, RR = $100,000.

$$4.15) \quad RR = r_r \, DD\sqrt{}$$

The reserve ratio requirement is in the denominator of the money multiplier. This indicates an inverse relationship between r_r and m. A higher reserve ratio requirement means a lower money multiplier. A lower money multiplier, in turn, results in a lower money supply. A lower reserve ratio requirement, by contrast, leads to monetary expansion.

The inverse relationship between r_r and m exists because reserve requirements restrict the amount of lending (and money creation) banks can potentially undertake. However, recent changes in the reserve ratio requirements for U.S. banks indicate that, for this country, r_r is less of a constraint on bank lending than it was in the past. These changes in U.S. reserve requirements, and their implications for the U.S. money multiplier, are described in Section C below.

iii) Excess Reserve Ratio: r_e

Reserve requirements specify minimum proportions of reserves to deposits. Banks are free to hold additional reserves, and often have. These additional reserves are called excess reserves. In equation 4.16), the volume of excess reserves (ER) is calculated as the difference between total reserves (R) and required reserves (RR).

4.16) ER = R - RR

Because excess reserves are nonearning assets, holding them reduces bank profits. Hence, banks must have an overriding motive if they are to hold any excess reserves. When they do so, it generally is because of uncertainties surrounding the management of their cash position. These problems relate to difficulties associated with forecasting deposit withdrawals and loan demand.

Banks do not know, with certainty, the amount of deposit withdrawals and loan demand that will occur on any given day. Both of these activities result in a reduction of a bank's reserve position. Consequently, banks must have a strategy for coping with these uncertainties. One such strategy is called asset management. This involves holding liquid assets in the bank portfolio. When pressures on the cash position do occur, these liquid assts serve as built-in shock absorber. Because excess reserves are the most liquid of assets, they sometimes are held for this purpose.

When banks hold excess reserves, those reserves are not available to support bank lending activity. From the perspective of bank lending (and the accompanying money creation), it is as if the reserves do not exist. That is, the holding of excess reserves reduces the potential size of the money supply.

It does so through the money multiplier. The excess reserve ratio (r_e) is in the denominator of the multiplier, indicating an inverse relationship. As banks hold more excess reserves, in relation to their checkable deposits $(r_e \uparrow)$, the money multiplier is smaller. A smaller value for m implies a reduction in M1. Reducing excess reserve holdings (relative to DD$\sqrt{}$), on the other hand, expands the money supply.

iv) A Numeric Example

The general public, commercial banks, and the government potentially influence the size of the money stock through the money multiplier, whose value depends on the levels of k, r_r, and r_e. k is determined by the behavior of the general public; r_e, by the behavior of commercial banks. In the U.S., r_r also is largely determined by commercial banks. That is the case even though the requirements originate through government.

Other things equal, all three are in an inverse relation to m. Assume, for example, that $k = .5$, $r_r = .05$, and $r_e = .05$.

$$4.17) \quad m = (1 + k) / (r_r + r_e + k) = (1.5) / (0.6) = 2.5$$

From equation 4.1) a multiplier of 2.5 indicates that the money supply is 2.5 times the level of the monetary base. Moreover, from equation 4.2), any change in the level of the monetary base results in a change in the money supply that is 2.5 times the change in the quantity of base money. This multiplier effect, which is the direct consequence of fractional reserve banking, has very important consequences for monetary policy. If bank reserves are increased through monetary policy, there will be a multiple expansion of bank deposits. A reduction in reserves leads to a multiple contraction of bank deposits. This phenomenon is known as the multiple expansion and contraction of bank credit.

II. General Instruments of Monetary Control

There are three general instruments of monetary policy: 1) open market operations;

2) the discount window/discount rate; and, 3) reserve ratio requirements. They are called

general instruments because their effects are widespread. That is, their usage has an

impact throughout the country, and across most markets. This has important political

implications, especially for democracies. In situations where monetary policy inflicts

economic hardship, it is more politically palatable (or considered a "fair game") if it

affects nearly everyone.

A. Open Market Operations

i) History

Open market operations are the purchase and sale of securities by the central bank.

They are by far the most important monetary-policy instrument in the U.S. today. This

was not always the case. Indeed, when the Federal Reserve Act was passed in 1913,

there was no understanding of this instrument. The Act did empower individual Reserve

Banks to purchase U.S. government securities and bankers acceptances. The motives

were twofold: 1) to allow Reserve Banks to earn additional income to cover operating

expenses; and, 2) to promote international trade.

The potential impact of such purchases (and sales) on economic activity was

discovered by accident in the early 1920s. This discovery led to the formation of a series

of committees within the Federal Reserve System. The motive was to coordinate security

purchases and sales by individual banks. If open market purchases and sales did

significantly affect the economy, an attempt to coordinate these actions made sense.

Ultimately, open market purchases and sales were codified into law with the Banking Acts of 1933 and 1935. The 1933 legislation provided for a Federal Open Market Committee (FOMC) that would assume responsibility for the conduct of open market operations. No longer were individual Banks allowed to purchase and sell securities. Instead, purchases and sales were done on behalf of all 12 Federal Reserve Banks. Individual Banks could refrain from participation, but that option was removed in the Banking Act of 1935.

ii) The Process

Open market operations originate with the FOMC, which meets approximately every six weeks. Intra-meeting decisions occasionally occur via conference call, but they are the exception. FOMC meetings include both the presentation of economic forecasts and policy discussion. They end with the issuance of a set of instructions (called a directive) to the Account Manager of the Federal Reserve Bank of New York. The directive is written in general terms, but the Account Manager is in attendance at the meetings to capture the intent of the Committee. The Account Manager then uses the directive to carry out open market operations on behalf of all twelve Reserve Banks.

Federal Reserve purchases and sales of securities occur via a process known as the "go around." Once the Account Manager decides a course of action, he (or she) informs traders at the New York Federal Reserve Bank. These traders, in turn, contact (or "go around" to) security dealer firms in the New York City money market. Actual trades are between the New York Fed and these dealer firms.

Assume, for example, that the Account Manager's decision is to buy a given quantity of U.S. government securities within a specific maturity range. Traders contact individuals at the security dealer firms and ask them if they have any such securities for sale. If they do, traders want to know how many and at what price? Dealer firms offering securities are asked if they are willing to hold firm on their offers for the next 30 minutes. All offers are posted at the New York Fed, and the decision is made to accept or reject the offers. Typically, the Fed buys securities with the lowest offer price (and the highest yield). Once the decision is made, traders again contact the security firms and inform them if their offers are accepted or rejected.

Most all U.S. open market operations involve secondary-market purchases or sales of U.S. government securities. Even though U.S. Treasury securities are exchanged, the U.S. Treasury (who issued the securities) is not involved. The Treasury issued these securities at some time in the past, and someone else now owns them.

The fact that open market operations are conducted in the secondary market for U.S. government securities has an important implication. They do not affect the overall size of U.S. government debt. What changes is the composition of ownership of U.S. Treasury debt. If the Fed purchases securities, more of the debt is now owned by Federal Reserve Banks, and less is owned by security dealer firms.

iii) Accounting for Open Market Operations

The monetary impact of open market operations is determined by how the transactions are financed. Purchases and sales by the Federal Reserve are paid for with *bank reserves*. Payment is made on a pass-through basis, and involves the Fed, a set of security dealer firms, and the clearing banks for the dealer firms.

The T-accounts associated with an open market purchase are presented in EXHIBIT 4.5. As a simplification, it is assumed that only one security dealer firm (Firm D) and one clearing bank (Bank D) are involved. The combined balance sheet for Federal Reserve Banks shows an increase in Treasury securities (TS) on the asset side. This records the acquisition of securities.

The offsetting entry is an increase in MBD on the right-hand (liability) side. MBD is total commercial bank deposits at Federal Reserve Banks. The increase in this item on the Fed's balance sheet indicates how the Federal Reserve paid for securities acquired in the open market purchase. The Fed does not directly pay the security

---

EXHIBIT 4.5

T-Accounts for Open Market Purchase

Federal Reserve Bk.		Bank D		Firm D	
TS +	MBD +	MBD +	DD√ +	DD√ +	
				TS -	

---

dealer firm (Firm D) but, instead, pays the clearing bank (Bank D) for the security dealer firm. It does so by increasing that bank's deposit balance at the Fed. Bank D then passes the payment through to dealer firm.

The pass-through payment is shown on the T-account for Bank D. This clearing bank now has a larger deposit balance at the Federal Reserve Bank, but also has an increase in its deposit liabilities (DD√). This increased checking account balance is owned by the security dealer firm (Firm D), and represents the pass-through payment from the clearing bank to Firm D. The T-account for Firm D now shows both the increase in its deposit balance at Bank D and a reduction in its holdings of U.S. government securities.

iv) Open Market Operations and the Money Supply

Commercial bank balances at Reserve Banks (or member bank deposits, MBD) count as bank reserves. When the Federal Reserve pays for securities by increasing these balances, the total volume of reserves in the banking system increases. Because banks need reserves in order to make loans, banks are now in a position to extend more credit.

This has important implications for the money supply. When banks make additional loans, the money supply increases. Indeed, in a world of fractional reserve banking, there will be a multiple expansion of bank credit. In the above example, the raw material for such a multiple expansion of bank deposit money appears in the form of additional bank reserves at Bank D.

The world of fiat money is a world of inflation, and this secular decline in the purchasing power of money largely is the consequence of government expansion of the money supply. For many market-oriented economies in the industrial world, expansion the money supply occurs mainly through such open market purchases. In these economies, open market operations now serve as the "printing press."

Open market purchases (and sales) of securities affect the base money equation (4.8). Federal Reserve purchases increase TS (a factor of increase), with the offsetting entry an increase in base money (B). In the basic money supply model (4.1), the increase in B results in an increase in M1. The multiple expansion of deposit money occurs through the workings of the money multiplier, which is larger than one in a world of fiat money and fractional reserve banking. The impact of those changes on equation 4.1) is shown below.

4.18)   M1 ($\uparrow$) = B($\uparrow$)m

v) Transmission of Bank Reserves

In this country, new reserves brought into the system via open market purchases are initially located in New York City banks. That is because open market operations are with dealer firms and clearing banks in New York City. Some of the new reserves may be used to support lending activity in this locale. However, reserves tend to follow economic activity and the newly created reserves can be used to support lending activity in any part of the country. Avenues for the transfer of these reserves from Bank D to other parts of the country (or world) are many. Only a few are mentioned here.

One possibility is that a New York City firm borrows money from Bank D and spends the proceeds of the loan outside the city. Another is that a firm outside New York

City borrows from Bank D and, likewise, spends the funds outside of New York City. Still another possibility is that the reserves will leave New York City through activity in the federal funds market. This last possibility is examined in more detail.

The federal funds market is one where immediately available (or same day) funds are loaned. These funds must be immediately available because many of the loans are for one day only. This market has long been a medium for the transfer of bank reserves. Activity in the market commenced in the early 1920s, with banks loaning reserves to one another on an overnight basis. The market flourished during the final third of twentieth-century, with many small banks joining the ranks of large banks by using the market as a medium for adjusting their short-term reserve positions. Some of the more aggressive larger banks commenced to use the market for more than simply adjusting their reserve position. The reserves they acquire are employed to support their long-term loan portfolios.

EXHIBIT 4.6 shows T-accounts for a typical federal-funds market transaction. In this example, Bank D loans reserves to Bank DBQ in Dubuque, Iowa. Bank D instructs the Federal Reserve to transfer a portion of its reserves to the account of Bank DBQ. When this happens, there is no change in the aggregate volume of commercial bank balances at Federal Reserve Banks. However, there is a change in the ownership composition of these balances. The Fed's balance sheet shows an increase in MBD_{DBQ} (Bank DBQ's balance) and a decrease MBD_D (Bank D's balance).

Bank D has swapped assets. Its balance sheet shows an increase in federal funds sold (FFS +) and a decrease in its reserve balance at the Fed (MBD_D -). The balance

---

EXHIBIT 4.6

Federal Funds Market Transaction

Bank D		Federal Reserve Bk.		Bank DBQ	
MBD_D –		MBD_D –	MBD_{DBQ} +	FFP +
FFS +		MBD_{DBQ} +		

---

sheet for Bank DBQ reflects its larger reserve balance at the Fed (MBD_{DBQ} +), and an increased liability for federal funds purchased (FFP +). The bank reserves created by the Fed's open market purchase now reside with Bank DBQ in Dubuque, Iowa.

B. Discount Rate/Discount Window

A second general instrument of monetary policy is the discount rate. This is the interest rate the Federal Reserve Bank charges banking institutions when they borrow reserves at the discount window. When the Federal Reserve System was initially organized in 1914, the country was still operating with fiduciary money (the gold standard). At that time, the discount rate was the principal instrument of monetary control. The U.S. was following in the footsteps of the U.K., where the bank rate of Bank of England had long been the centerpiece of monetary policy. But, there was more to it than that. Open market operations were not understood in 1914, and reserve ratio requirements were set by statute. Hence, the discount rate was the *only* general instrument of monetary control.

Individual Reserve Banks set the discount rate with the approval of the Federal Reserve Board. There were many instances, early in the history of the Federal Reserve System, when the discount rate was not uniform across all Federal Reserve Districts. That is uncommon today, where a uniform discount rate policy across Federal Reserve Districts reflects the high degree of integration of financial markets in the U.S.

For decades, the Federal Reserve has employed non-price rationing in managing the discount window. This was due, in part, to prolonged periods where the discount rate was set below the federal funds rate. To limit bank borrowing through the discount window, the Fed established rules and guidelines for appropriate commercial bank use of the discount window. These rules and regulations were known as the Federal Reserve's "administration" of the discount window. The Fed made it known that banks should use the discount window mainly as a means of managing their short-term reserve position. Continuous borrowing was frowned upon and considered a violation of Fed policy.

The Federal Reserve recently changed its discount window policy. Regulation A was revised in a manner that eliminated much of the non-price rationing at the discount window. The Fed increased the discount rate by 150 basis points, and placed it 100 basis points above the federal funds rate. All banks in sound condition, and with adequate collateral, now are permitted discount-window borrowing at their own discretion. With the discount rate above the federal funds rate, banks generally are expected to adjust their reserve positions in the federal funds market.[40]

---

[40] For a summary of these changes in discount rate policy, see Ed Stevens, "The New Discount Widow," *Economic Commentary,* Federal Reserve Bank of Cleveland, May 15, 2003.

During the first two decades of the Federal Reserve System, the discount window was a major source of bank reserves and of variation in the monetary base. The proportion of reserves coming through the discount window did not fall below 37 percent in the 1920s, and was in excess of 80 percent in 1921. During this period, changes in the discount rate were of major significance. That is no longer the case. With the ascendance of open market operations as the primary instrument of policy, the importance of the discount window has steadily diminished.

Today, the ratio of borrowings at the discount window to total bank reserves most often is less than 0.1 percent. This indicates that virtually none of the current bank reserves are coming through the discount window. Although this is an overstatement, current changes in the discount rate are tantamount to a price change in a market where there is no activity.

While the significance of the discount rate has diminished, officials of the Federal Reserve are not ready to abolish the discount window. It can play a major role when the Fed assumes the posture of lender of last resort. The central bank plays that role in situations that could result in financial panic. Two more recent incidents were the stock market crash in 1987, and the terrorist attacks on the New York City Twin Towers in 2001. During such episodes, the Federal Reserve often is desirous of making sizable volumes of bank reserves available on short notice. The discount window is well suited for this purpose.

Both open market purchases and lending through the discount window provide additional reserves to the banking system. From a policy perspective, however, they differ in one critical respect. In the case of open market purchases, the Federal Reserve takes the initiative. For loans through the discount window, individual commercial banks must initiate activity. That is, nothing happens until a bank approaches the Fed and requests a loan.

T-Accounts for a discount window loan appear in EXHIBIT 4.7. Bank A requests and receives a loan from a Federal Reserve Bank. The loan appears in the Fed's balance sheet as an increase in D (Discounts and Advances). The proceeds of the loan are made available to Bank A in the form of an increased deposit balance at the Federal Reserve Bank. Hence, MBD_A increases on the right-hand side of the Fed's balance sheet.

Bank A owns that deposit balance, which shows as a left-hand side entry in its balance sheet (MBD_A +). The offsetting entry is on the liability side (D +). This additional liability reflects Bank A's obligation to repay that loan at a later date.

Discounts and Advances (D), from the Fed's balance sheet, are a factor of increase

---

EXHIBIT 4.7

Discount Window Loan

Federal Reserve Bk.				Bank A			
D	+	MBD_A	+	MBD_A	+	D	+

---

in the Base Money Equation (4.8). Hence, a discount-window loan increases the level of monetary base. Repayment of the loan has the opposite effect. It decreases the monetary base. The affect that increased lending through the discount window has on the money supply is seen in equation 4.19) below. Again, with fractional reserve banking, an increase in base money results in a multiple expansion of deposit money.

$$4.19) \qquad M1(\uparrow) = (B \uparrow) m$$

C. Reserve Ratio Requirements

Banking started as individual proprietorships or partnerships that were unregulated. Today, most banks are corporations that are very heavily regulated by government. Reserve requirements are one form of government regulation. These regulations specify that commercial banks must hold reserves in some minimum proportion to bank deposit liabilities.

When the Federal Reserve Act was passed in 1913, reserve requirements were set by statute. The Banking Act of 1935 gave the Federal Reserve Board the authority to set (and change) reserve requirements for all federally chartered banks. The Depository Institution Deregulation and Monetary Control Act of 1980 extended the Federal Reserve's authority to cover all depository institutions---both bank and nonbank, and state chartered as well as federally chartered depository institutions.

Unlike open market operations and lending through the discount window, changes in reserve requirements do not affect the total volume of reserves in the banking system. Historically, changes in reserve requirements affected the maximum amount of deposits a given volume of reserves could support. When reserve requirements were increased, available bank reserves would potentially support a smaller quantity of deposits. A decrease in reserve requirements had the opposite effect. Available reserves could now potentially support a larger quantity of bank deposits.

Changes in reserve requirements have been infrequently used as a means of adjusting monetary policy. For that reason, they have been a minor instrument of monetary policy. Recently, many banks in the U.S. commenced new banking practices (with sanction from the Federal Reserve) that further diminished the significance of reserve requirements.

Beginning in 1994, these commercial banks began to reclassify a portion of their checkable deposits liabilities as money market deposit accounts (MMDAs). Such reclassifications, referred to as sweeps, were motivated by the desire to limit the impact of reserve ratio requirements.[41] Because they were done only for reserve accounting purposes, sweeps did not alter the nature of the securities owned by bank customers. However, banks employing sweeps now had two sets of books (or balance sheets). One set was for reserve accounting; the other, for general dissemination.

Use of sweeps effectively lowered a bank's reserve requirements. The reason is that checkable deposits were subject to reserve requirements, while MMDAs were not.[42] By reducing the bank's level of checkable deposits (for reserve accounting purposes), sweeps had the effect of reducing a bank's required reserve holdings. The same level of

---

[41] For a discussion of sweeps and their implications, see Richard G. Anderson and Robert H. Rasche, "Retail Sweep Programs and Bank Reserves, 1994-1999," *Review*, Federal Reserve Bank of St. Louis, January/February, 2001, pp. 51-72.

[42] Exclusion from reserve requirements was an important feature of MMDA deposits, which were created in the Garn-St. Germain Act of 1982. However, there was an important qualification attached to this exclusion. No more than six withdrawals were allowed per month. If this qualification was not met, an MMDA deposit was treated as a transactions account (subject to reserve requirements applicable to those accounts).

checkable deposits now called for fewer required reserves. Banks using these sweeps had, in effect, lowered their own required reserve ratio. The bank's new required reserve ratio was below the one specified by the Federal Reserve.

Critical features of these new reserve ratio requirements are summarized below:

- For banks using sweeps, the reserve requirement ratio is not the one stated by the Federal Reserve. It is below the Federal Reserve's reserve ratio requirement.
- Because required reserves are calculated from a different set of bank liabilities than those reported to the public, the new reserve requirement is not visible to the general public.
- The reserve requirement is determined by individual banks, although it is conditioned by the Federal Reserve's official reserve requirement.
- The reserve requirement varies by bank, and can differ for banks with identical liability structures (but different sweeps).
- Changes in reserve requirements set by the Federal Reserve may elicit little response from the banking system.

Given the implications for monetary policy, the last feature requires elaboration. Following sweeps, the new lower reserve requirement is not a binding constraint for many banks. The reserves they choose to hold to meet customer demands for credit, and for potential adverse check clearings, are above the level of required reserves. For banks in such a position, an increase or decrease in the Federal Reserve's reserve requirements is likely to leave them in a similar position. That is, their required reserves are still below those they choose to hold for normal banking operations. As a consequence, the change in the Fed's reserve requirements may have no impact on the bank's level of desired reserve holdings and lending policies.

With reserve requirements for many banks below those specified by the Fed, and with the Federal Reserve's reserve requirements having only a negligible impact on many banks, an alternative version of the base money multiplier is more appropriate for the

181

U.S. economy. It focuses attention on total reserve holdings of banks instead of partitioning them into required and excess reserves. Thus, it differs slightly from the money multiplier in 4.9) above.

Let $r = r_r + r_e$, where r is an aggregate reserve ratio for banks. Given the Federal Reserve's diminished role in establishing reserve requirements, r is largely determined by commercial bank behavior. With the currency ratio (k) determined by the behavior of the general public, the size of the reconstituted money multiplier (in 4.20 below) is largely determined by the behavior of economic agents in the private sector.

$$4.20) \quad m = (1+k) / (r+k)$$

III. Closed Market Operations

From a global perspective, most money creation is not based on the three policy instruments discussed above. The largest share of the world's fiat money is created in less developed countries and/or countries that embraced socialism. Open market operations are not an option for these countries because financial markets are so poorly developed.[43]

Poorly developed markets certainly have not hampered their ability to create money. They are responsible for creating nearly all the world's fiat money, which is accomplished through a process called closed market operations.

---

[43] The absence of an adequate financial infrastructure may result from the fact that these countries are poor. It may not. These countries may be poor because of a weak market structure. Their governments, in many cases, have actively discouraged the development of markets. It should come as no surprise that these countries can not rely upon markets for the implementation of monetary policy.

Monetary policy in these countries is a by-product of (government) Treasury financing operations. Governments wish to spend more money than they obtain in tax revenues. Because there is no active market for Treasury securities, selling bonds in the open market is not an option. Instead, the Treasury issues new bonds and places them directly with the central bank. The central bank pays for these securities by crediting the deposit account of the Treasury at the central bank. The Treasury now is in a position to spend more.

The T-accounts for this closed market operation are in EXHIBIT 4.8. The Treasury balance sheet shows an increase in its cash balance at the central bank (TRD +). The increase in Treasury liabilities (TS +) are for bonds (or Treasury Securities) placed with the central bank. The balance sheet for the central bank shows that this institution now owns more Treasury securities (TS +). The offsetting entry is the increase in the Treasury's deposit balance (TRD +) with the central bank.

Once the Treasury spends these new cash balances, Treasury deposits at the central

---

EXHIBIT 4.8

Closed Market Operations

Treasury				Central Bank			
TRD	+	TS	+	TS	+	TRD	+

---

bank (TRD) are transformed into bank reserves (MBD). Banks are now in a position to extend additional credit. Massive amounts of fiat money are created in this fashion.

APPENDIX A

Derivation of the Base Money Equation

The base money equation is an accounting identity. It is derived from two other identities: 1) the balance sheet for the central bank; and 2), the Treasury Monetary Account. These identities summarize the monetary influences of the central bank and the Treasury respectively.

The derivation here is for the U.S. monetary system. Variables in the base money equation reflecting Federal Reserve policy are from the combined balance sheet for all 12 Federal Reserve Banks. EXHIBIT 4.9) presents that balance sheet. Equation 4.21) shows the identity between total Federal Reserve assets and the summation of total liabilities and capital accounts for Federal Reserve Banks.

$$4.21) \quad TS + D + CIPC + FE + GC + SDRC + TC_{FRB} + OFRA \equiv FRN_P + FRN_T + FRN_B + MBD + TRD + FD + DACI$$

U.S. Treasury activities influence the quantity of base money in several ways. It issues that portion of circulating currency (Treasury currency, or TC) which is in the form of coins. The Treasury also holds the vast quantities of gold (G) owned by the U.S. government. It is also the repository for Special Drawing Rights (SDRs) owned by the U.S. government. SDRs are a form of bookkeeping money issued by the International Monetary Fund to individual countries. They are used exclusively to settle payments imbalances between countries.

Gold and SDRs holdings of the U.S. government have monetary significance

EXHIBIT 4.9

Combined Balance Sheet for Federal Reserve Banks

Assets	Liabilities

(TS) U.S. Treasury Securities
(D) Discounts and Advances
(CIPC) Cash Items in the
     Process of collection
(FE) Foreign Exchange
(GC) Gold Certificates
(SDRC) Special Drawing Right
     Certificates
(TC$_{FRB}$) Treasury Currency
     Held by Federal Reserve
     Banks
(OFRA) Other Assets minus
     Other Liabilities and
     Capital Accounts
	Federal Reserve Notes:
	  (FRN$_P$) owned by the public
	  (FRN$_T$) owned by the Treasury
	  (FRN$_B$) owned by commercial banks
	
	Deposits:
	  (MBD) owned by commercial banks
	  (TRD) owned by the Treasury
	  (FD) owned by Foreign Central Banks
	     and International Institutions
	
	(DACI) Deferred Availability
	     of Cash Items

when the Treasury monetizes them. It does this by issuing claims on these assets to the Federal Reserve Banks. Gold certificates (GC) are claims on the government's gold holdings; Special Drawing Rights Certificates (SDRC), claims on the government's SDR balances. In exchange for these ownership claims issued to the Federal Reserve, the Treasury receives an increase in its cash balance at Federal Reserve Banks (TRD). When such an exchange occurs, Gold and/or SDRs have been monetized. Once the Treasury spends these new cash balances, bank reserves (R) and bank deposit money (DD√) increase.

The Treasury Monetary Account (4.22) captures the impact of these Treasury operations on the money supply. It is assumed that 100 percent of the gold and SDR holdings of the Treasury are monetized. It follows that $G = GC$ and $SDR = SDRC$. Currency (or coins) issued by the Treasury (TC) are partitioned into those by owned by banks, the general public, and Federal Reserve Banks respectively.

4.22) $G + SDR + TC \equiv GC + SDRC + TC_B + TC_P + TC_{FRB}$

> where, G = gold holdings of the Treasury
> SDR = Special Drawing Rights held by the Treasury
> GC = Gold Certificates owned by the Federal Reserve
> $SDRC$ = Special Drawing Right Certificates owned by the Federal Reserve
> TC = Treasury Currency issued
> TC_B = Treasury Currency owned by banks
> TC_P = Treasury Currency owned by the general public, and
> TC_{FRB} = Treasury Currency owned by Federal Reserve Banks

The base money equation is obtained by aggregating equations 4.21) and 4.22) and, then, solving for base money. Initially, the left-hand side of both equations is summed and is equated to the summation of the right-hand side of these equations.

4.23) $TS + D + CIPC + FE + GC + SDRC + TC_{FRB} + OFRA + G + SDR + TC \equiv$
$FRN_P + FRN_T + FRN_B + MBD + TRD + FD + DACI + GC + SDRC + TC_B$
$+ TC_P + TC_{FRB}$

Several substitutions are made to simplify this identity. Federal Reserve float (F) is defined as $CIPC - DACI$, and entered on the left-hand side. TCH (Treasury Cash Holdings) is substituted for FRN_T. GC, SDRC, and TC_{FRB} appear on both sides of the identity. Consequently, they cancel. The result is identity 4.24).

4.24) $TS + D + F + FE + G + SDR + TC + OFRA \equiv FRN_P + TCH + FRN_B$
        $+ MBD + TRD + FD + TC_B + TC_P$

The remaining task is to solve for base money (B), which is equal to $R + C$. Employing the Federal Reserve's definition, bank reserves (R) are equal to total bank vault cash (or, $TC_B + FRN_B$) plus aggregate commercial bank balances at Federal Reserve Banks (MBD). Currency in circulation outside banks (C) is equal to $TC_P + FRN_P$. Hence, $B = TC_B + FRN_B + MBD + TC_P + FRN_P$. Collecting these terms and transposing the others yields the base money equation.

4.25) $B = TS + D + F + FE + G + SDR + TC + OFRA - TCH - TRD - FD$

APPENDIX B

Derivation of the Base Money Multiplier

The basic money supply model (equation 4.26) relates the level of the monetary base to the level of the money supply. Connecting the two is the base money multiplier. The money multiplier (m) is the number which, when multiplied times the level of base money (B), yields the money supply (M). In a world of fiat money with fractional reserve banking, the value of the money multiplier is greater than one. The size of the multiplier varies with the measure of money under consideration. The multiplier derived here is for the M1 measure of money.

Several assumptions are employed. First, a multi-bank system is assumed. Second, the reserve ratio requirement (r_r) is contemporaneous and fixed. It applies only to checkable deposits (DD√). Finally, the excess reserve (r_e) ratio and the currency ratio (k) also are fixed. All three of these ratios, which are discussed in pages 162-167 above, are presented as equations 4.27) - 4.29).

4.26) $M = B (m)$

4.27) $r_r = RR / DD√$

4.28) $r_e = ER / DD√$

4.29) $k = C / DD√$

> where RR is aggregate required reserves,
> ER is aggregate excess reserves, and
> C is total currency in circulation outside banks.

As indicated in 4.30), base money (B) is measured as summation of total bank reserves (R) and total currency in circulation outside of banks (C). Total bank reserves, in turn, are partitioned into required reserves and excess reserves.

4.30) $B = R + C = RR + ER + C$

From equations 4.27) – 4.29), the following substitutions are made: $r_r(DD\sqrt{})$ is substituted for RR; $r_e(DD\sqrt{})$ for ER; and, $k(DD\sqrt{})$ for C.

4.31) $B = r_r(DD\sqrt{}) + r_e(DD\sqrt{}) + k(DD\sqrt{})$

$= (r_r + r_e + k)DD\sqrt{}$

Solving 4.31) for $DD\sqrt{}$ yields 4.32). This expression for $DD\sqrt{}$ is substituted into 4.33), an equation for the M1 measure of money. The result is 4.34), the basic money supply model for M1-money. The term in brackets is the money supply multiplier (m).

4.32) $DD\sqrt{} = B / (r_r + r_e + k)$

4.33) $M1 = DD\sqrt{} + C = DD\sqrt{} + k(DD\sqrt{}) = (1 + k)DD\sqrt{}$

4.34) $M1 = B [(1+k) / r_r + r_e + k]$

Given recent changes in the reserve ratio requirements in this country, an alternative version of the multiplier is more appropriate for the U.S. economy. It is the

190

multiplier in 4.20) above. This multiplier uses an aggregate reserve ratio (r) for banks.

That is, let $r = r_r + r_e$. Substitution of r into 4.34) yields this second money multiplier.

4.35) $m = (1 + k) / (r + k)$

CHAPTER 5

MONEY AND INCOME

I. Fisher's Equation of Exchange 193

II. Velocity and the Demand for Money 196

III. Money and the Economy 198

    A. The Liquidity Trap 199

    B. Money and Real GDP 200

    C. The Quantity Theory Money 201

IV. Some Didactic Exercises..203

    A. Secular Deflation 204

    B. Secular Price Stability 205

    C. The Quantity Theory of Money 206

    D. Hyperinflation..206

I. Fisher's Equation of Exchange

The equation of exchange was the mechanism employed by Irving Fisher to analyze the relationship between money and economic activity.[44] The basis for the equation was the proposition that there are two sides to every transaction: a buyer and a seller. Aggregating across all transactions, the total value of all things bought (B) is exactly equal to the total value of all things sold (S).

$$5.1) \qquad B \equiv S$$

The right-hand side of the relationship is the goods side. The total value of all things sold (S) is equal to the sum of the price times the quantity for each item sold. Fisher wrote this as PT, where P is the average price and T is the total number of transactions. PT, then, is substituted for S on the right-hand side of equation 5.1).

The left-hand side is the money side. In a strictly monetary economy, all things are sold for money (M). However, it is not possible to substitute M for B on the left-hand side of 5.1) because it is very unlikely that each unit of money was used exactly once in financing all exchanges (PT).

What relates money to spending is the velocity of circulation of money. Velocity (V_T), or transactions velocity, is the average number of times each unit of money is used in financing PT. It is now possible to represent total expenditures for goods and services

---

[44] The source for Fisher's analysis is: Fisher, Irving, *The Purchasing Power of Money* [Fairfield, NJ: Augustus M. Kelley, 1913 (Reprinted 1985)].

as MV_T, and this term is substituted for B in equation 5.1). The result is Fisher's version of the equation of exchange.

5.2) $MV_T = PT$

One problem with this version of the equation of exchange is that it is not operational. Fisher advanced the equation prior to the development of our system of national income accounts. Subsequent to the development of these accounts, Fisher's equation was modified to a form that was operational.

5.3) $MV = Py$

where   M is the money supply,
            V is income velocity of money,
            P is the average price of all final
                goods services sold, and
            y is the number of final goods and
                services sold

Modern governments measure both the money supply (M) and nominal gross domestic product (GDP). But, the right-hand side of 5.3) is nominal GDP. With measures for both M and Py, it is possible to calculate velocity (V). Consequently, this modified version of the equation of exchange is fully operational and, for that reason, generally is preferred to Fisher's statement of the equation of exchange.

Before proceeding, this modified version (which is subsequently employed) is compared to Fisher's version. Py, or nominal GDP, is a measure of all final goods and services currently produced. Fisher's PT is the total value of all goods and services currently exchanged. Because many goods and services currently exchanged are not currently produced, Py is a proper subset of PT. That is, every good or service currently produced is contained in PT. Many things currently exchanged (and in PT), however, were produced in the past. Hence, they are not included in GDP. One such example is the sale of a used automobile.

With the same money supply (M), and with Py different from PT, the velocity terms in 5.2) and 5.3) are not the same. For that reason, they are represented by different symbols. Fisher's V_T is the number of times (on average) money is used in all exchanges. V, on the other hand, is the average number of times each unit of money is used in the financing of GDP expenditures. Because Py is smaller than PT, V is smaller than V_T.

Fisher's equation of exchange was criticized on the grounds that it was a tautology. Fisher's response was that just because a relationship is a tautology does not mean that is without value. The equation of exchange is a case in point. Even though it is a tautology, it is a very useful device for analyzing factors responsible for changes in the purchasing power of money.

Based on the equation of exchange, all changes in the purchasing power of money are the result of changes in M, V, y, or some combination of the three. The reason is that if P (and 1/P) change, something else in the equation of exchange must have changed as well. Otherwise, MV ≠ Py.

Increases in M bring about increases in P. Thus, they reduce the purchasing power of money (1/P). Increases in P are also occasioned by the more frequent use of money. Hence, like M, V and the purchasing power of money are also indirectly related.

Increases in production (y), however, have the opposite effect. A greater quantity of goods, with the same amount of money, leads to lower prices for goods. That is the same thing as an increase in the exchange value of money. To summarize, M and V are indirectly related to the purchasing power of money, while y is directly related.

II. Velocity and the Demand for Money

Cambridge University economists in England developed the theory of money in a manner that did not involve the equation of exchange. A.C. Pigou, for example, began his analysis by treating money like any other good. From his perspective, there is a market for money, and his approach was to analyze the supply and demand for money within that context. He was able to derive several money-spending relationships that were similar to those of Fisher.[45]

No detailed analysis of differences in the two approaches is undertaken here.[46] However, it is important to note the relationship between the demand for money and Fisher's velocity of circulation of money. The two are inversely related to one another. When individuals increase their demand for money, they tend to hold money for a longer period of time, and the velocity of circulation of money falls. Likewise, reductions in the demand for money tend to increase velocity. Individuals are spending money more frequently.

---

[45] For Pigou's version of the quantity theory of money, refer to A.C. Pigou, "The Value of Money," *The Quarterly Journal of Economics*, 32 (November, 1917), 38-63.
[46] One important distinction is that the Cambridge demand for money is a static concept. It typically applies to a given point in time. By contrast, Fisher's velocity of circulation of money happens over a period of time.

Derivation of that inverse relationship is shown in equations 5.4) - 5.6). Note that velocity is a relative measure of the demand for money. It reveals how much money individuals collectively demand in relationship to GDP. Moreover, the relationship is in inverse form.

5.4) $V = (Py) / M$

5.5) $V^{-1} = 1/V = M / (Py)$

In monetary equilibrium, the quantity of money supplied (M) is equal to the quantity of money demanded (M^d). Hence, M^d is substituted for M in equation 5.5). Because individuals demand real (not nominal) money balances, the numerator and denominator on the right-hand side of equation 5.5) are both divided by the average price (P). The resulting relationship between velocity and the demand for real money balances is stated in equation 5.6).

5.6) $1/V = (M^d/P) / y$

When individuals collectively demand more real money balances in relationship to real GDP (y), velocity falls. Relative reductions in real money demand result in an increase in the velocity of circulation of money.

III. Money and the Economy

The equation of exchange is also useful in analyzing the relationship between money and the economy. If the money supply changes, the offsetting entry in the equation of exchange must be either V, P, or y (or some combination of the three). Those three possibilities are shown in Exhibit 7.1.

Exhibit 7.1

Absorption of Money Changes Within the Equation of Exchange

	M	V	=	P	y
A. Liquidity Trap	↑	↓			
B. Money and Real GDP	↑↓				↑↓
C. Quantity Theory of Money	↑↓			↑↓	

A. The Liquidity Trap

If increases in the money supply are absorbed in the form of a reduction in velocity, we are experiencing what John Maynard Keynes described as absolute liquidity preference. In this case, monetary policy has no effect on aggregate spending because individuals hold rather than spend any increase in the quantity of money. Keynes considered this case a theoretical curiosity: "Whilst this limiting case might become practically important in the future, I know of no example of it hitherto."[47]

While Keynes may have discounted its importance, that was not the case for his disciples (Keynesians). Rejecting Keynes' reticence, they renamed the phenomenon the liquidity trap and raised it to the level of a general case. The liquidity trap was something that routinely occurs during business cycle downturns. One of the more dramatic episodes, according to the Keynesians, was the Great Depression. During that cataclysmic decline, velocity decreases thwarted efforts by the Federal Reserve to end the depression through increases the money supply.

When Keynesian economics attracted more followers in the 1950s and 1960s, the concept of the liquidity trap gained credibility. This had enormous policy implications. For, if monetary policy is unreliable, its policy role is necessarily a secondary one. The ensuing relegation of monetary policy to the background made possible the major acceleration of money growth and inflation that plagued the U.S. economy in the 1960s and 1970s.

The discovery that activist economic policies lead to more inflation, and not higher living standards, placed followers of Keynes on the defensive. As Keynesian economics

---

[47] Keynes, John Maynard, *The General Theory of Employment, Interest, and Money* (New York: Harcourt, Brace & World, 1936), p. 207.

lost credibility, so, too, did the concept of the liquidity trap. Significant in its demise were research findings published by Milton Friedman and Anna Schwartz in *A Monetary History of the United States* (1963).

An important component of their study was the construction of a money supply series for the U.S. back to 1860. These data led Friedman and Schwartz to reject the Keynesian interpretation of the Great Depression. The U.S. economy was not caught in a liquidity trap in the 1930s. In contrast to Keynesian assertions, it was not a situation where individuals were holding rather than spending Fed-induced increases in the money supply. The data revealed, instead, an unprecedented decline in the stock of money, which fell by 35 percent from 1929-1933. With a lack of empirical support for the existence of a liquidity trap, the concept was unceremoniously relegated to the position originally assigned to it by Keynes.

B. Money and Real GDP

If changes in money are not absorbed by changes in velocity, they affect spending. Through their impact the right-hand side of the equation of exchange, they bring about changes in the level of nominal GDP. Such changes in nominal GDP can, in turn, be further decomposed into changes in the average price (P), real GDP (y), or both.

Economists such as Irving Fisher, R.G. Hawtrey, and, more recently, Milton Friedman argue that money affects spending differently in the short-run than in the long-run. In the short-run, changes in money primarily affect real magnitudes such as the level of production (y) and the employment of resources. Because money is considered the main cause of business cycle fluctuations, these economists have what is called a monetary theory of the trade cycle. With fiat money controlled by central banks, it is governments that are the primary source of economic instability. It follows that the best prospect for taming the business cycle is for governments to provide greater monetary stability.

The long-run impact of changes in money is primarily on prices. This money-price nexus, nourished historically by numerous cases of government's debasement of money, has a rich tradition. One of the earliest episodes involved the Roman emperor, Nero, but the tradition is a robust one. It transcends different types of money and different forms of government. This long-run relationship between money and prices is formally known as the quantity theory of money.

C. The Quantity Theory of Money

The quantity theory of money is a misnomer. It is not a theory of money. Rather, it is a theory about what determines the long-run purchasing power of money. Fisher employed his equation of exchange as a mechanism to explain the quantity theory. It deserves mention that the equation of exchange, alone, is a tautology and not a theory. Hence, it is not sufficient to state that M and P are directly related to one another in the equation of exchange, *ceteris paribus*. That, too, is a tautology.

To develop his version of the quantity theory of money, Fisher augmented the equation of exchange with two additional assumptions.[48] First, he argued that, in the long-run, changes in the money supply do not affect the velocity of circulation of money.

---

[48] In an attempt to simplify Fisher's macroeconomic anlysis, some state that he assumed that velocity and real output are held constant. That is incorrect. For a discussion of this mischaracterization of Fisher's analysis, see William D. Gerdes, "Mr. Fisher and the Classics," *The American Economist*, Spring 1986, 66-72.

Other factors, however, do. He cited urbanization, changes in commercial customs (such as the use of credit), and changes in technology (e.g., improved transport) as causing velocity to change in the long-run. Hence, velocity was not a constant. It just wasn't affected by the money supply.

Second, in the long-run, changes in the money supply do not affect the level of production (y). If they did, we would have a guaranteed remedy for world poverty. Simply send printing presses to poor countries, and let print massive quantities of fiat money. In fact, many of them have already tried this, to no avail. The reason why this does not work is obvious. Printing additional fiat money does not increase wealth. Indeed, in many cases, it does the opposite.

The observation that money does not affect production in the long-run does not imply that production is a constant. Long-run production obviously does change. According to Fisher, factors responsible for long-run increases in production are increased availability of resources and improvements in technology.

Fisher's two assumptions are summarized in equations 5.7) and 5.8).

5.7) $dV/dM = 0$

5.8) $dy/dM = 0$

If money does not affect either V or y, it must affect P. That gives rise to Fisher's version of the quantity theory of money. Simply stated, in the long-run, a given change in the money supply occasions a direct and equiproportionate change in the average price (relative to what it otherwise would have been).

Two things deserve mention here. First, while Fisher's quantity theory of money is a tautology as a theoretical exercise, it is not so empirically. It is possible for long-run changes in money to be reflected in something other than the average price. They could potentially be absorbed by velocity changes or changes in production.

Second, Fisher's theory does not state that long-run movements in M and P are equal to one another. The long-run movement in P is a resultant of the combined effects of changes in M, V, and y. While all three do have an influence, they are not all equally important. Fisher emphasized the relative importance of changes in money, which is a trademark of those in the quantity theory tradition.

IV. Some Didactic Exercises

Hitherto, Fisher's quantity theory of money was stated in terms of levels. To state that theory in terms of growth rates, a dynamic version of the equation of exchange is required. That version is presented in equation 5.9) below. The reconstituted quantity theory of money is as follows. A given change in the growth rate of money (dM/M) occasions a direct and equiproportionate change in the growth rate of the average price (dP/P) relative to what it otherwise would have been.

5.9) $dM/M + dV/V = dP/P + dy/y$

Below are several didactic exercises employing this dynamic version of Fisher's theory. Numeric examples associated with these exercises appear in Exhibit 7.2

A. Secular Deflation

The U.S. experienced secular deflation in the last one-third of the nineteenth century. This was a period of rapid industrialization in the country, and the growth rate for production was high by historical standards. The country was on the gold standard, and there were no new major discoveries of gold from mid-century until the late 1890s. As a consequence, production growth exceeded the growth rate for money. The result was a secular increase in the purchasing power of money.

Secular deflation of this type is portrayed as Case I in Exhibit 7.2. Real GDP is growing 4 percent per year, while the money supply is unchanged. Assuming no secular trend in velocity, the average price falls at the annual rate of 4 percent.

This scenario has an important implication. Inflation is not a necessary condition for economic growth. By increasing the availability of goods and services, economic

---

Exhibit 7.2

Dynamic Version of the Equation of Exchange

	dM/M	+ dV/V	=	dP/P	+ dy/y
Case I	0	0		-4	4
Case II	4	0		0	4
Case III	1,500	500		2,000	0

growth is actually *deflationary*. This deserves mention because the myth that inflation is necessary for growth was popular among development economists in the past half century. Some contemporary economists, and members of the popular media, often expound a similar view. Alarmed when the U.S. inflation rate falls below two percent, they agonize about the potential dire consequences of deflation. The nineteenth-century U.S. experience provides a good historical counterexample for those harboring such thoughts.

B. Secular Price Stability

For a country to experience secular price stability, money growth should approximate the long-run growth of production. That occurs in Case II, Exhibit 7.2. Both money growth and production growth are 4 percent per annum. Assuming no secular growth in velocity, the result is secular price stability.

Long-run price stability does not imply that prices are stable every year. For some years, an economy might experience inflation; for others, deflation. But, for longer periods of time, the average price is stable. This was the U.S. experience with commodity and fiduciary monies. In 1933, the average price was approximately the same as it was in the early 1780s. (Refer to Chapter 1, page 26, for a graph of the average price in the U.S. during this period.) Such long-run price stability with commodity or fiduciary money is not unexpected. Market forces, under these arrangements, tend to bring about money growth rates that conform to the growth rate of production. For a more detailed discussion, see pp. 99-101.

C. The Quantity Theory of Money

The dynamic version of the quantity theory is demonstrated by moving from Case I to Case II in Exhibit 7.2. The growth rate of money increases by 4 percent---from zero percent in equation Case I to 4 percent in Case II. The rate of change for prices also increases by 4 percent. Initially prices are falling at a rate of 4 percent per year. After the acceleration in money growth, the growth rate for the average price is zero percent, or 4 percent higher than it was before. While the quantity theory implies that the increase in the growth rate of the average price equal the increase in the growth rate of money, note that it does not imply that the growth rates of money and the average price are the same.

D. Hyperinflation

Hyperinflation occurs when prices increase extremely rapidly. There is no threshold inflation rate where hyperinflation commences. Nevertheless, hyperinflation is generally not difficult to identify. It occurs under fiat money regimes, and can last for more than one year. However, it is not a long-run phenomenon. The process typically comes to an end when the government responsible for the hyperinflation announces that it is undertaking "monetary reform." The reform usually assumes the form of a new fiat money. It is physically different from the previous fiat money, and often has a new name, e.g., the real as opposed to the peso. A rate of exchange of the old for the new currency is announced (x-"kazillion" units of the old for one unit of the new). There were numerous such episodes in the twentieth-century.

Case III, Exhibit 7.2, is a numeric example of what happens during hyperinflations. The central bank increases the money supply at the rate of 1,500 percent a year. With the money side of the equation of exchange increasing at this rate, great stress is transferred to the right-hand side of that equation. That stress is dissipated in the form of massive increases in prices.

This stress on the goods side (or right-hand side) of the equation of exchange is exacerbated by the behavioral response of owners of money balances. With hyperinflation, transactions costs in the form of storage costs for money increase dramatically. Simultaneously, large changes in relative prices are occurring, and everyone becomes an inadvertent speculator. The kind of portfolio adjustments individuals make in this environment matters a great deal. One type of portfolio adjustment, however, is not speculative. The purchase of almost any type of good is preferred to the ownership of money, and virtually all individuals soon learn to minimize their holding period for money balances. The result is a massive increase in the velocity of circulation of money. In case III, the increase is 500 percent per year.

Reflecting pressures from both M and V, the annual inflation rate is now 2,000 percent. Although not portrayed in this example, the disruptive influence of this degree of monetary instability often leads to a significant decline in production (y). While very small when compared to the influences of M and V, this fall in production further erodes the purchasing power of money.

With M, V, and y all exerting upward pressure on P, the real money supply (or M/P) actually falls during hyperinflations. For those who focus on the real money supply, this can lead to the perverse interpretation that the economy is experiencing "tight money."

CHAPTER 6

MONETARY POLICY

I. Monetary Policy in a World of Fiat Money 209

    A. Effects of Fiat Money...210
        i) Monetary Nationalism...210
        ii) Inflation 211
        iii) Reduced Services of Money.................................213
        iv) Lower Economic Growth.................................215

II. Expansion of Fiat Money: Motives...216

    A. Seigniorage 217
        i) The Seigniorage Tax...218
        ii) Maximum Seigniorage 219
        iii) Hyperinflation...221

    B. Macroeconomic Management 226

III. Discretionary Monetary Policy 228

    A. Transmission Mechanisms 228

    B. Choice of Monetary Targets.................................232

    C. Interest Rate Targeting in the U.S.................................233

I. Monetary Policy in a World of Fiat Money

Most of man's accumulated experience is with commodity money. Fiduciary money, by contrast, is relatively new. It has only been with us for the last several centuries. Like commodity money, the origin of fiduciary money generally is viewed as a spontaneous market development. The supposition is that the process that led to both of these types of money involved attempts by individual economic agents to reduce the transactions costs associated with voluntary exchange.

Nearly all money in use today is fiat money. As largely a twentieth-century phenomenon, this is a relatively new form of money. Unlike the other two types of money, the adoption of fiat money was not a spontaneous market development. It mainly came about through coercive acts of governments. Those undertaken by the U.S. government in 1933 are a case in point. President Roosevelt, acting on authority granted by Congress, issued an executive order making it illegal to hold monetary gold, with all outstanding monetary gold confiscated through forced exchanges.[49] These actions effectively eliminated the convertibility option of the existing fiduciary money arrangement. Contracts relating to money ownership were not the only ones affected. All other contracts (such as bonds) written in terms of monetary gold were, likewise, summarily voided.

While individual economic agents generally preferred fiduciary money to fiat money, governments clearly did not.[50] The convertibility option associated with fiduciary

---

[49] Banks, businesses, and individuals had three weeks to turn in their gold to the government. There were limited exceptions. Individuals could keep $100 in gold coins; coin collectors were allowed two specimens for any issue. So much gold was confiscated, that the U.S. government deemed it necessary to construct a large vault at Fort Knox, Kentucky. For a discussion of the U.S. nationalization of gold, refer to Chapter 12 in Jack Weatherford, *The History of Money* (New York: Three Rivers Press, 1997).

[50] Had consumers preferred fiat money, issuers would have provided it volitionally. As noted, absence of the convertibility option makes life easier for issuers of money.

money significantly constrained government control over money. The reason was that excessive issue of fiduciary money threatened the integrity of the convertibility option, raising the specter of financial panic. Elimination of the convertibility option removed that constraint, and gave individual governments the freedom to issue money at will.

With less than a century of continuous usage of fiat money, our relative lack of experience gives us a limited window for assessing the consequences of government control of money. One thing about fiat money, however, is abundantly clear. Under government control, changes in the quantity of money are not a random process. Decisions by governments across the world have led to unprecedented increases in the quantity of money.

A. Effects of Fiat Money

Despite our limited experience with fiat money, enough time has passed to permit a few tentative generalizations relating to its usage.

i) Monetary Nationalism

The adoption of fiat money accomplished its major objective. Governments now have much greater control over money. Instead of a global monetary system integrated by the use of a common money (or monies), we now have monetary nationalism. With a few exceptions, each country has its own money. Each of these monies is loosely linked to one another by activities in foreign exchange markets. Under this arrangement, individual countries are free to employ that particular monetary policy that best suits policymakers in the country. This was a major motive for moving away from fiduciary money. In this respect, then, the adoption of fiat money was a success.

ii) Inflation

While national governments have much greater monetary autonomy in a world of fiat money, virtually all of them have used their monetary sovereignty in a similar manner. They have increased the quantity of fiat money. As a consequence, all countries share a common experience: inflation. The inflation has been continuous and, in many cases, pronounced. As a result, the period since the adoption of fiat money has appropriately been dubbed the age of inflation.

Data assembled by economic historians suggest that this title is well deserved. Rates of inflation that followed the adoption of fiat money are without precedent. David H. Fischer identifies four great inflations of the past millennium: the medieval inflation, the 16th century inflation, the 18th century inflation, and the 20th century inflation.[51] Each of these inflations was widespread as evidenced by its impact on residents in many different countries. Inflation data for England, which generally conform to the experience of other countries, are presented in TABLE 6.1. Note that the rate of price increase during the 20th century inflation far exceeds that for any of the other three great inflations. Average annual inflation in twentieth-century England was more than three times the average inflation rate for the 16th and 18th century inflations, and nearly seven times the average inflation rate recorded during the great medieval inflation.

---

[51] Fischer, David Hackett, *The Great Wave: Price Revolutions and the Rhythm of History* (New York: Oxford University Press, 1996).

TABLE 6.1

Four Great Inflations in England
(Average Annual Inflation Rate)

I. Medieval Inflation (1265-1360)	0.6
II. 16th Century Inflation (1475-1650)	1.3
III. 18th Century Inflation (1730-1810)	1.3
IV. 20th Century (1900-2002)	4.1

Sources: E.H. Phelps Brown and Sheila V. Hopkins,
"Seven Centuries of the Prices of Consumables, compared
with Builders' Wage-rates," *Economica*, 23, November,
1956, 296-314. Data for 1954-2002 are from
International Financial Statistics: Yearbook, various
issues

The preeminence of the twentieth century inflation, in terms of magnitude, is even more remarkable when one considers that fiat money was only widely adopted about one-third of the way through the century. As a consequence, most of the twentieth century inflation accrued in the last half of the century. Average annual inflation in the United Kingdom, for example, was 6.5 percent from 1960-2002. Numerous other countries experienced double-digit average inflation for this period. These data leave little doubt that the other three great inflations pale by comparison with 20th century inflation.

The effects of twentieth-century fiat money inflation on the purchasing power of money have been devastating. TABLE 6.2 shows the cumulative decline in the purchasing power of money in each of 55 countries for the 42 year period from 1960-2002. Note the breadth of the inflation experience. Massive depreciation in the exchange value of money occurred in all 55 countries. None fared better than Panama and Germany, where money only lost more than two-thirds of its value. The median country on the list is Portugal, where money lost 98.5 percent of its exchange value. In 26 of the countries, money lost in excess of 99 percent of its purchasing power.

iii) Reduced Services of Money

The plummeting exchange value of the world's currencies has important implications for the services provided by money. Throughout the world, money has largely ceased to serve as a store of value. This is manifested differently in various parts of the world. In the United States, individuals hold money balances almost exclusively for transactions purposes. Wealth accumulation occurs primarily via other assets such as stocks, bonds, and real assets.

In the less developed countries, on the other hand, one frequently observes a plethora of partially completed homes. The decision to build a home in stages, and over a period of years, is grounded in economic logic. Given the depreciation in the purchasing power of money in those countries, the poor of the world would never achieve home ownership through savings accumulated in the form of money balances.

TABLE 6.2

Percent Depreciation in Value of Money: 1960-2002

Panama	67.2	Angola	99+
Germany	72.4	Argentina	99+
Japan	81.5	Bolivia	99+
United States	83.5	Brazil	99+
Canada	84.5	Chile	99+
France	88.1	Colombia	99+
Morocco	89.3	Costa Rica	99+
Norway	89.5	Ecuador	99+
Sweden	89.9	Ghana	99+
Australia	90.0	Israel	99+
Denmark	90.4	Mexico	99+
Finland	91.1	Nicaragua	99+
Cameroon (62)	92.7	Nigeria	99+
United Kingdom	92.9	Paraguay	99+
Ireland	94.1	Peru	99+
Italy	95.2	Poland (70)	99+
Rwanda (66)	95.4	Romania (70)	99+
India	95.7	Russia (92)	99+
Spain	96.4	Sudan	99+
Burundi (64)	96.7	Tanzania (65)	99+
Swaziland (65)	97.2	Turkey	99+
South Africa	97.4	Uganda (81)	99+
Egypt	97.5	Uruguay	99+
El Salvador	97.5	Venezuela	99+
Korea	98.0	Zaire/Rep. Congo(63)	99+
Kenya	98.1	Zimbabwe (65)	99+
Philippines	98.2		
Portugal	98.5		
Greece	98.6		

Source: *International Financial Statistics* (various issues), International Monetary Fund.
Note: Data series for some countries begin after 1960. Starting dates for those countries are indicated by parentheses, e.g., Zimbabwe (65)

In the more extreme cases of inflation, money often is rejected as a medium of exchange. The transactions costs associated with using the country's money are deemed excessive. In rejecting the money of their own country, individuals sometimes select that of another country (such as U.S. dollars) for use as an exchange medium. This phenomenon is known as currency substitution. An alternative to currency substitution is reversion to barter. Even though the transactions costs associated with barter are often relatively high, in these cases, they are lower than when using money.

In responding to the monetary chaos they have created, governments often call in the old currency and replace it with a new currency. The rate of exchange can involve thousands of units of the old currency for one unit of the new. Because the old currency is discredited in a major way, it is common to give the new currency new colors and a new name. Once implemented, such "monetary reform" positions government to once again expand the quantity of fiat money at its own discretion.

iv) Lower Economic Growth

Fiat money has been a vehicle for the transfer of massive quantities of resources from the private sector of the economy to government. This is especially true in many less developed countries, where money growth rates are relatively high. Historically, unpopular means such as taxation or other coercive measures have been the principal method for governments to increase their ownership of resources. The ability to print fiat money has given them an attractive alternative. By spending the money that they create, governments are able to wrest resources away from individuals without having recourse to more direct forms of coercion.

This additional source of finance has permitted twentieth-century governments to become much larger. A major consequence of the adoption of fiat money, then, is that it greatly enhanced the economic power of government relative to that of individuals. Given that more rapid economic growth generally is associated with greater individual economic freedom and more secure property rights, widespread use of fiat money has, no doubt, led to a reduction in world economic growth (relative to what it otherwise would have been). Because the alternative is a path not taken, it is difficult to know the magnitude of the reduction in living standards.

II. Expansion of Fiat Money: Motives

Our current age of inflation is a direct result of adopting fiat money. With inflation largely orchestrated by governments, the question of motivation arises. Is it in the self-interest of governments to expand the quantity of fiat money? The answer to this question is in the affirmative. Self-interested governments are driven by two principal motives.

One is seigniorage, or government revenue from money creation. Government control of money has permitted a significant reallocation of resources---from the private sector of the economy to government. Consequently, the world of fiat money is not only a world of inflation, but also one characterized by the rapid growth of government.

The second motive is found mainly among governments in several of the relatively industrial and market-oriented economies of the world. Influenced by the writings of British economist John Maynard Keynes, these governments have used monetary policy as a tool in the attempt to control movements in the aggregate economy. These efforts have resulted in significant money creation accompanied by inflation.

A. Seigniorge

The motive for most increases in the world money supply is seigniorage. Governments around the world consume vast quantities of resources. One way for them to wrest these resources from the private sector is taxation. As noted above, however, taxation generally is politically unpopular. Moreover, many governments of the world do not have fiscal systems in place that generate the quantity of tax revenues necessary to finance their desired expenditure programs. This is especially true in less developed countries, where greater use of currency in effectuating exchanges, more limited voluntary tax compliance, and the lack of legitimacy significantly hamper government's quest for tax revenues.

An alternative to taxation is for government to finance expenditures by printing money. This can assume several forms. First, government can simply print new currency and spend it. There are numerous historical examples of this. One occurred during the Revolutionary War in this country, when the Continental Congress authorized the printing of currency (Continentals) to pay soldiers and to finance other wartime expenditures.

A second form is where the Treasury issues new bonds and places them directly with the central bank. In return, the Treasury receives an increase in its cash balance at the central bank. When the Treasury spends this additional cash balance, the quantity of money in circulation rises. This form of money creation is described as closed market operations in Chapter 4. It is popular throughout much of the world, and accounts for the bulk of fiat money creation.

A third, and more subtle form, is when the central bank monetizes debt issued by the Treasury. This is mainly possible in countries (such as the U.S.) that have encouraged the development of open financial markets. Monetizing debt occurs when the Treasury finances its expenditures by issuing bonds in the market. Those purchasing the newly issued bonds lose cash balances. The central bank replenishes this loss of private-sector cash balances through an open market purchase (equivalent in value to the Treasury bond sales). This joint Treasury/central bank venture results in additional Treasury cash balances at the central bank with no (net) loss of cash balances in the private sector. When the Treasury spends its new cash balances, the money supply increases.

i) The Seigniorage Tax

Printing money is posed as an alternative to taxation. It, too, however, is a form of taxation. Unlike other taxes, though, it is a hidden or covert tax. The burden of this tax is borne by holders of (real) money balances. They are not presented with a tax bill but, instead, find that the additional inflation occasioned by government money creation adversely affects their money holdings. These cash balances now purchase fewer goods and services than they did before, i.e., their real cash balances have decreased.

The nominal seigniorage (S), in this case, is the money value of the goods and services that government is able to buy with the money it prints. Assuming that all money is government money, nominal seigniorage is equal to the increase in the money supply (dM, where dM > 0). Equation 6.1) shows the level of nominal seigniorage.

6.1) $S = dM$

6.2) $s = dM/P = (dM/M)(M/P)$

The quantity of goods and services (dM/P) the government can actually purchase with this new money is the real seigniorage, or s. In equation 6.2), real seigniorage is written as the product of the rate of growth of the money supply (dM/M) and the quantity of real money balances (M/P). This permits us to see more clearly the genesis of real seigniorage.

(dM/M) (M/P) is the level of the seigniorage tax on holders of real money balances. To demonstrate this, recall Fisher's quantity theory. A given growth rate for money increases the growth rate of prices by the same proportion. That is, $dM/M = d(dP/P)$. A 10 percent rate of money growth, for example, causes dP/P to be 10 percent higher than it otherwise would have been. Thus, real money balances depreciate by ten percent more than they otherwise would, or by dM/M.

In 6.2), then, the growth rate of money is the tax rate that is applied to the quantity of real money balances, the tax base. The product of the two is the amount that real money balances fall as a consequence of money creation. This tax on holders of real money balances is precisely equal to the (real) government revenue from money creation, or s.

ii) Maximum Seigniorage

The maximum amount of seigniorage government can collect is complicated by the fact that taxpayers are sensitive to tax rates. In this case, rational economic agents reduce their desired holdings of real money balances as inflation increases. That is, as

the tax rate increases, the tax base declines. In equation 6.2), increases the growth rate of

money (dM/M ↑) result in lower holdings of real money balances (M/P ↓).

Whether additional money creation increases real seigniorage depends on the

relative strength of these two opposing forces. The tax rate elasticity of the tax base is

the appropriate measure of this.

6.3) $\eta = d(M/P)/(M/P) / d(dM/M)/(dM/M)$

TABLE 6.3 shows the various possibilities. If $\eta > -1$, the numerator is smaller

(in absolute terms) that the denominator. Hence, the tax base is changing less rapidly

than the tax rate. In this case, increases in the growth rate of money result in higher real

seigniorage.

If (in absolute terms) the tax base changes more, in proportionate terms, than does

the tax rate, $\eta < -1$. This is the third case in TABLE 6.3. The increased sensitivity of

taxpayers to tax rates means that a higher growth rate for money now results in less real

seigniorage. A government desirous of more seigniorage must now reduce the growth

rate of money.

It follows that a government interested in maximizing real seigniorage should

increase the growth rate of money up to the point where $\eta = -1$. At this point, the

(proportionate) increase in the tax rate is exactly offset by the (proportionate) decline in

the tax base. Further increases in the growth rate of money reduce real seigniorage.

In Figure 6.1 below, maximum seigniorage occurs with tax rate $(dM/M)_2$.

TABLE 6.3

Money Growth and Seigniorage

	dM/M	s
$\eta \; > \; -1$	↑	↑
$\eta \; = \; -1$	↑	→
$\eta \; < \; -1$	↑	↓

iii) Hyperinflation

Inflation can degenerate into hyperinflation, or a very high rate of inflation. When this happens, inflation can reach hundreds or even thousands of a percent per month. There have been numerous instances of hyperinflation, and all are associated with the use of fiat money. Without the constraint imposed by a convertibility option, governments are free to create massive quantities of money. Some have chosen to do so.

Data from some of the major twentieth-century episodes of hyperinflation are presented in TABLE 6.4. One of the most dramatic cases occurred in Hungary immediately after World War II. Inflation averaged 19,800 percent per month for nearly one year. To grasp the magnitude of this inflation, consider the impact on the price of a candy bar selling for $1. With this inflation rate, the price would increase to nearly eight million dollars in three months.

TABLE 6.4

Episodes of Hyperinflation

Country	Dates	Average Inflation Rate (per month)
Germany	Aug. 1922-Nov. 1923	322
Greece	Nov. 1943-Nov. 1944	365
Hungary	Aug. 1945-July 1946	19,800
Poland	Jan. 1923-Jan. 1924	81
Russia	Dec. 1921-Jan. 1924	57

Source: Phillip Cagan, "The Monetary Dynamics of Hyperinflation," in *Studies in the Quantity Theory of Money*, ed. by Milton Friedman, University of Chicago, 1956.

Hyperinflation occurs when a government's quest for seigniorage becomes dynamically unstable. Government prints more money in order to spend more. But, the ensuing inflation means that government is actually able to purchase fewer goods and services than before. Therefore, the government prints even more money. This results in even higher inflation, again reducing the purchasing power of the money created by government. Additional money is created, and the acceleration of money growth eventually spirals out of control.

The massive quantities of money created by government put enormous upward pressure on prices. In terms of Fisher's equation of exchange [6.4) below], both M and P are increasing dramatically. But, a second factor is exacerbating the spiraling inflation.

The rapid increase in prices constitutes a sharp rise in the tax on holders of real money balances. Individual owners of money respond rationally by reducing their cash holdings. These reduced money holdings are manifested in the following way. People experiencing hyperinflation spend money nearly as quickly as they receive it. The result is very rapid increase the velocity of circulation of money.

6.4) $M V = P y$

$\uparrow \uparrow \quad \uparrow$

Not only are rapid increases in M causing prices to soar, but increases in velocity are pushing prices even higher. With M and V both exerting upward pressure on P, P increases more than M. That is, real money balances are falling. While that is the intent of the general public (as owners of money balances), it is a significant part of the problem confronting government. Government is creating money because of its purchasing power. By increasing velocity, the behavior of the general public is destroying that purchasing power.

At the epicenter of this dialectic is a level of desired real seigniorage that is inconsistent with the public's preferred holdings of real money balances. While government controls the nominal quantity of money, it does not control the quantity of real money balances. The latter is the result of portfolio decisions made by the general public.

A graphical version of this dialectic appears in FIGURE 6.1. Each point on the seigniorage curve associates a level of real seigniorage with a given growth rate for

FIGURE 6.1

Seigniorage with Hyperinflation

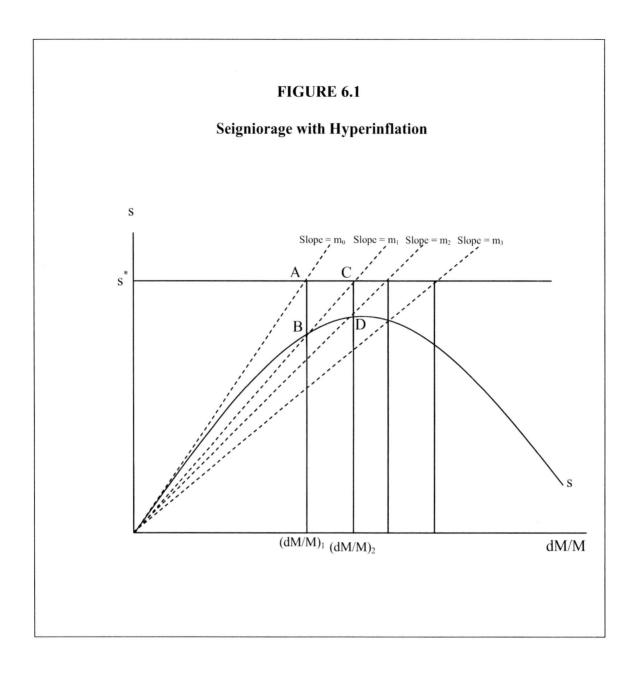

money.[52] As is indicated in equation 6.2), what relates these two variables is the level of

---

[52] This seigniorage curve is discussed in J. Huston McCulloch, *Money and Inflation: A Monetarist Approach* (2nd. Edition), New York: Acacemic Press, 1982. He refers to it as a monetary Laffer curve, and notes that it was introduced by Martin Bailey long before the concept was employed by Arthur Laffer. See Martin Bailey, "The Welfare Cost of Inflationary Finance," *Journal of Political Economy,* April, 1956.

real money balances held by the public. Real seigniorage (s) is equal to the product of the growth rate of money and the level of real money balances. Money supply growth is the government-controlled tax rate, while the level of real cash balances is the tax base determined by the general public. For any given growth rate for money, there exists a *desired* level of real money balances for the general public. The product of the two yields the real seigniorage accruing to government when the general public is holding its desired real money balances. The seigniorage curve in FIGURE 6.1 is a locus of such points.

For a fixed level of actual real money balances (as opposed to a desired level), the graph of equation 6.2) becomes a linear relation with actual real money balances serving as the slope. Each level of money supply growth is proportionate to an associated level of real seigniorage. Several such linear rays are shown in FIGURE 6.1. Each corresponds to a different fixed level for real money balances. The declining slopes ($m_0 > m_1 > m_2 > m_3$) signify falling real money balances.

Each point where a linear ray intersects the seigniorage curve (e.g., B and D) is an equilibrium point. The public's desired holdings of real money balances (embedded in s) is equal to actual real money balances reflected in the slope of the linear ray. For all other points, disequilibrium obtains. In those instances, actual real money balances differ from desired holdings.

Assume that the government's desired real seigniorage is s*. The initial level of actual real money balances is m_0. The government increases the money supply growth to $(dM/M)_1$ in order to generate s* (at point A). At point A, however, the inflation rate occasioned by that money growth rate causes owners of real money balances to

225

collectively reduce their holdings of real cash balances to the desired level (m_1) associated with that tax rate.[53] Real seigniorage falls to point B.

To reach its desired seigniorage, government now accelerates money growth to $(dM/M)_2$. In FIGURE 6.1, the movement is along the ray (with slope m_1) from point B to point C. The higher inflation rate associated with $(dM/M)_2$ again causes owners of real money balances to reduce their holdings, this time to m_2. The higher inflation and reduced money holdings again thwart government. Real seigniorage falls to point D. Again the government responds. Note that each time government accelerates money growth, real money balances are reduced, with ultimate result of hyperinflation.

B. Macroeconomic Management

For several of the world's relatively industrial and market-oriented countries, seigniorage is not the principal motive for government increases in the quantity of fiat money. Instead, governments have increased the money supply in an effort to achieve macroeconomic objectives such as increased economic growth, more moderate economic fluctuations, and reduced unemployment.[54]

Monetary policy employed for this purpose is called discretionary monetary policy, because central banks in these countries change the policy at their own discretion. Such discretion was very limited under fiduciary money arrangements, but has blossomed with the adoption of fiat money. Indeed, the abandonment of the gold standard in the twentieth

---

[53] To simplify the analysis, other influences on money demand (such as interest rates and income) are assumed to be fixed.

[54] Other types of economic policy are available for use by governments. They include fiscal policy, exchange-rate policy, and wage and price controls. The focus here is on monetary policy.

century was largely motivated by the desire of governments to have greater flexibility in the management of monetary policy.

The objectives of governments employing discretionary policy have varied. Some viewed discretionary monetary policy as a means to stimulate higher economic growth, although this goal is seldom mentioned today. On the other hand, virtually all governments now state long-term price stability as a major policy goal. A primary objective for devotees of discretionary monetary policies remains, however, the attempt to moderate short-term business cycle fluctuations.

This emphasis on short-term business fluctuations is more suitable to modern governments, where bureaucrats often possess short-term time horizons. It dates back to the confluence of three related events in the 1930s that provided the impetus for governments to more actively engage in discretionary economic policies. Those events were the Great Depression, the abandonment of the gold standard, and the influence of the writings of British economist John Maynard Keynes.

Keynes argued that moderating fluctuations would contribute in a significant way to improving material living standards. Moreover, he was confident that a judicious employment of government economic policies could accomplish this. On the monetary side, what were required were appropriate doses of monetary simulation and restriction. Stimulation was necessary when the economy lagged; monetary restriction, when an economy became overheated.

While use of monetary policy for this purpose is symmetrical in theory, it has not been in practice. Government policies have been heavily biased toward monetary stimulation. The result has been significant monetary expansion accompanied by secular inflation.

III. Discretionary Monetary Policy

Discretionary monetary policy is most feasible in countries such as the U.S., where financial markets are both relatively open and more highly developed. Central banks in these countries adjust policy instruments in response to perceived changes in the economic environment. Often those changes in policy instruments are directed toward influencing target variables that, in turn, affect ultimate policy objectives such as aggregate output or the price level. Such procedures require knowledge of the monetary policy transmission mechanism, which specifies linkages between the policy instruments, policy targets, and the objectives of monetary policy. In the U.S., the Federal Reserve's operational transmission mechanism relies upon interest rate targets.

A. The Transmission Mechanism

Knowledge of the transmission mechanism is essential for implementing activist monetary policies. This mechanism indicates, usually in a sequential fashion, how changes in the instruments of monetary policy actually bring about changes in economic activity. Views of economists differ concerning the nature of these linkages. Behind their disagreements are different theories of this monetary process. While an extensive discussion of alternative transmission mechanisms is not undertaken, two of the more conventional ones are presented. They are outlined in EXHIBIT 6.1.

```
┌─────────────────────────────────────────────────────────────────────┐
│                                                                       │
│                          EXHIBIT  6.1                                 │
│                                                                       │
│                     Transmission Mechanisms                           │
│                                                                       │
│                                                                       │
│   Model    Policy         Operating      Intermediate    Policy       │
│            Instrument     Target         Target          Objective    │
│   ──────────────────────────────────────────────────────────────     │
│                                                                       │
│                                                                       │
│     I      OMO →→→→→→  i_st   →→→→→  r_lt  →→  Py {P or y }            │
│                                                                       │
│                                                                       │
│    II      OMO →→→→→→  B   →→→→→  M  →→  Py {P or y }                  │
│                                                                       │
│                                                                       │
└─────────────────────────────────────────────────────────────────────┘
```

Monetary policy is initiated through the use of policy instruments. The instrument

variable in both of these transmission mechanisms is open market operations (OMO).

These operations are undertaken to affect the level of an operating target. The operating

target, in turn, affects the level of the intermediate target which influences the ultimate

objective (or objectives) of monetary policy. The objective variable for both

transmission mechanisms is nominal income (Py), which can be decomposed into its

component parts. They are the price level (P) and real output (y).

What differentiates the two transmission mechanisms are the targets employed.

One uses an interest rate target; the other, a monetary aggregate target. The first

transmission mechanism (Model I) employs an interest rate target. Use of interest rate targets has a long tradition among central banks. The bank rate has long been the centerpiece of monetary policy in England. Since its inception in 1913, Federal Reserve Banks in the U.S. have, for the most part, employed interest rate targets. Such targets have found favor with central banks in other countries, too.

This historical predilection by central banks for interest-rate targeting received twentieth-century theoretical support from Keynesian economists. Economists in this tradition argued that monetary policy primarily affects aggregate spending through its impact on interest rates. Given that such a perspective readily lends itself to interest rate targeting, the first transmission mechanism subsequently is referred to as the "Keynesian" transmission mechanism.

The operating target in this transmission mechanism is the short-term nominal interest rate (i_{st}). In the U.S., this short-term rate is the federal funds rate. In other countries, it is a comparable overnight rate. According to the theory, open market purchases increase the supply of loanable funds and push i_{st} downward. Open market sales have the opposite effect.

Changes in the operating target, in turn, affect the *long-term real* rate of interest (r_{lt}) in the same direction. The real interest rate is the intermediate target because the objective is to affect real spending (y). If rational economic agents think in real terms, and not nominal, terms, it is the real rate that must change.

Not only is the intermediate-target a real interest rate, but it also is a long-term rate. The objective is to affect spending on (business and consumer) durable goods, which are the most cyclically-volatile component of real aggregate spending (y). If the objective monetary policy is to "tame" the business cycle, it must have an impact on expenditures for these types of goods. The relevant rate of interest for durable goods expenditures, of course, is the long-term rate.

According to Model I, then, open market purchases lower the short-term nominal interest rate which, in turn, reduces the long-term real interest rate. A lower long-term real interest rate encourages spending on durable goods. Higher capital goods expenditures increase the level of real GDP. Open market sales have the opposite impact. Tighter monetary policy increases nominal and real rates and reduces real aggregate expenditures for durable goods.

Model II of the transmission mechanism uses monetary aggregates as targets. The immediate target is the quantity of base money; the intermediate target, the money supply. It is called the "classical" transmission mechanism because it focuses on the relationship between quantity of money and aggregate spending. This money-spending nexus has long been the center of attention for economists in the quantity-theory tradition.

In the case of Model II, open market purchases increase the quantity of bank reserves and the monetary base. An increase in base money leads to an increase in the money supply as banks use the newly-created reserves to extend their lending activity. Increases in the money supply, in turn, result in higher nominal spending. That is, nominal GDP increases. Open market sales initiate the opposite sequence that ultimately leads to a decline in nominal GDP.

Two features of this transmission mechanism deserve notice. First, the linkages in this transmission mechanism are concepts encountered before. The linkage between quantity of base money (the operating target) and the money supply (the intermediate target) is the base money multiplier. The velocity of circulation of money, of course, links the quantity of money (the intermediate target) and the level of nominal GDP (objective variable).

Second, while the changes in open market operations ultimately affect nominal GDP, it is the impact on the composition of GDP that is of greatest interest. Although many (in the quantity theory tradition) acknowledge that changes in money affect real GDP in the short-run, it is long-term consequences of changes in money that most concerns them. Maintaining long-run price stability and, thus, the "integrity" of money is the primary goal of monetary policy.

B. Choice of Monetary Targets

A target employed in the conduct of discretionary monetary policy generally must satisfy following two criteria. First, the target must be a variable that the central bank can control. Second, the target must be linked in a predictable way to the ultimate objective or objectives of policy.

The second criterion ultimately rests with "correctness' of the theory underlying the transmission mechanism. The importance of correctly specified linkages becomes apparent when considering the implications for targets that are not selected. Selection of an interest rate target, for example, implies the rejection of monetary aggregates as targets. In this case, the growth rate of the money supply becomes a "residual." Money is permitted to grow at whatever rate is necessary in order to maintain the interest rate target. Such neglect of money growth worries economists in the quantity theory tradition because it may lead to greater inflation.

Alternatively, targeting a monetary aggregate (such as base money) means that interest rates are free to fluctuate. This is an issue for proponents of Model I. From their perspective, greater variability in interest rates is likely to result in larger fluctuations in expenditures for durable goods and less macroeconomic stability.

The decision by the Federal Reserve in the U.S. to use interest rate targets reflects the Fed's judgment that interest rate targets better satisfy the two criteria stated above than do monetary aggregates. A critique of that judgment is presented in Chapter 7.

C. Interest Rate Targeting in the U.S.

Countries using interest rate targeting generally employ an overnight loan rate as the target. In the U.S., that rate is the federal funds rate. The federal funds rate is the interest rate charged on loans of immediately available funds. Such funds are also known as same-day funds because borrowers have access to the funds on the day of the loan. This is necessary for federal funds transactions because most are one-day loans.

A sizable portion of the activity in the federal funds market involves the lending of bank reserves owned by commercial banks and held at Federal Reserve Banks. Such loans involve the transfer of ownership of these reserve balances from one bank to another. Repatriation of these balances occurs when the loan is repaid.

The Federal Reserve System in the U.S. has used the federal funds rate as a target for decades. Only for a brief interlude (1979–1983) did the Fed switch to targeting monetary aggregates. Since that time it has continuously targeted the federal funds rate.

When the Federal Reserve uses this target, it does not actually set the federal funds rate. Commercial banks are free to negotiate loans of federal funds at any mutually agreeable interest rate. As an illustration of how federal funds rate targeting works, consider FIGURE 6.2 below. Each plot shows the daily trading range for the federal funds rate.

The initial target is 3%. In maintaining that target, the Federal Reserve permits the federal funds rate to fluctuate between 2.75 % and 3.25 %. Its task is to provide reserves to the banking system in quantities that will cause banks to price federal funds loans in the 2.75% to 3.25% range. If, for example, there is excess demand for federal funds when the rate is 3.25%, the Federal Reserve must make up this deficiency by providing more reserves to the federal funds market. It does so through open market purchases of

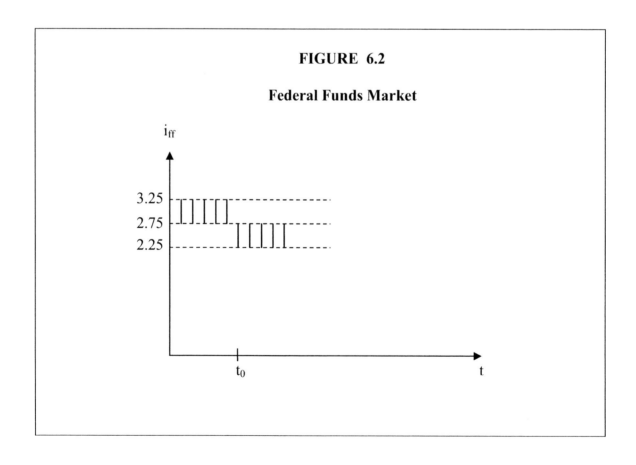

FIGURE 6.2

Federal Funds Market

U.S. Treasury securities. By accommodating the excess demand for federal funds, the freely-negotiated federal funds rate does not rise above 3.25%.

On the other hand, if there is an excess supply of federal funds at the 2.75% federal funds rate, the Federal Reserve must intervene to keep this freely-negotiated rate from falling below 2.75%. To decrease the quantity of reserves in the market, the Federal Reserve must undertake open market sales of Treasury securities. The media often describes this activity as: "The Fed drained reserves from the banking system."

A change in Federal Reserve policy is brought about by changing the level of the federal funds rate target. A higher target signifies tighter monetary policy; a lower target, monetary ease. Assume, in this example, that the central bank lowers the target from 3% to 2.5%. This occurs at time t_0 in FIGURE 6.2. The Fed must now provide a volume of reserves that keeps the federal funds rate between 2.25% and 2.75%. It accomplishes this through more liberal provision of reserves to the federal funds market, i.e., through increased open market purchases.

A graphical version of this policy change appears in FIGURE 6.3, where the federal funds rate is plotted against the quantity of federal funds supplied and demanded. The initial federal funds target was 3%. The lower federal funds rate target of 2.5% is achieved through an increase in the supply of federal funds. The supply curve shifts from S_0 to S_1 as a consequence of open market purchases by the Federal Reserve.

Two caveats related to interest rate targeting are mentioned here. First, the supply of money becomes a "residual" in the monetary process. The growth rate of the money is whatever rate is necessary to maintain the interest rate target. As noted above,

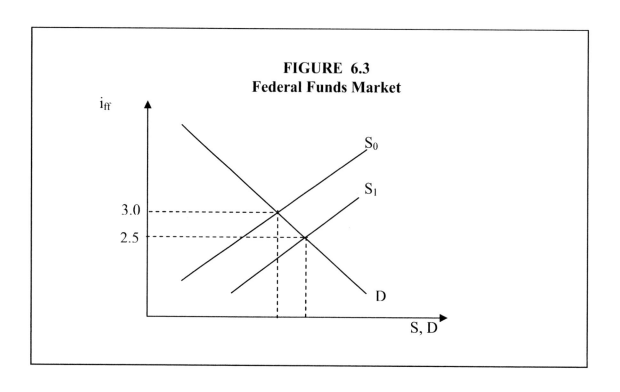

FIGURE 6.3
Federal Funds Market

adopting this approach has the potential for kindling or accelerating inflation.

Second, the ability of a central bank to successfully implement interest rate targeting is affected by the state of inflationary expectations. This was a problem for the Federal Reserve in the 1970s. In FIGURE 6.2, excess demand for federal funds at the rate of 3.25% caused the Fed to increase the supply of reserves through open market purchases. If this increase in bank reserves (and the accompanying increase in money growth) occasions an upward revision of inflationary expectations, the result is an even greater demand for bank reserves. Excess demand pressures reappear. To keep the rate from rising above 3.25%, the Federal Reserve must again provide additional reserves to the banking system. The growth rate of the money supply again increases, and impacts further on inflationary expectations.

In this scenario, interest rate targeting gives rise to dynamic instability in credit markets. It is driven by inflationary psychology, but fueled by central bank money creation. Once inflationary psychology becomes entrenched, an increase in the interest rate target may not signify monetary restraint. It may be a manifestation of prior monetary ease.

CHAPTER 7

CRITIQUES OF MONETARY POLICY

I. Interest Rate Targeting...**239**

    A. The Nominal/Real Dichotomy...**240**

    B. The Term Structure Problem..**245**

    C. A Recent U.S. Case Study...**246**

II. Friedman: Rules vs. Discretion...**250**

    A. Politics **251**

    B. Ignorance...**252**

    C. Friedman's x-Percent Money Growth Rule **255**

III. Rational Expectations **257**

IV. The Austrian Perspective..**259**

V. Postscript **267**

CRITIQUES OF MONETARY POLICY

From an historical perspective, fiat money is a relatively new phenomenon. That our experiences with this type of money have not been an unmitigated success is not surprising. Fiat money is controlled by government, and governments around the world generally are not noted for providing high-quality goods and services. Money is no exception.

Monetary policy is reasonably transparent, however, and the monetary performance of government has not gone without criticism. The critiques of government control of money discussed below are not concerned with situations where seigniorage is the principal motivation of monetary authorities. Rather, the focus is on the practice of discretionary monetary policy in countries where macroeconomic management is the driving force behind policy.

A common thread in these critiques is the issue of knowledge. More precisely, it is the lack of knowledge on the part of central bankers who carry out discretionary policy. There are other obstacles to the effective implementation of discretionary policies and they, too, are examined. Among them are the political environment of monetary authorities, adaptive behavior on the part of economic agents, and impact of monetary policy on the informational content of prices.

I. Interest Rate Targeting

Central banks in relatively advanced countries generally employ interest rate targeting to implement discretionary monetary policy. Excluding the four-year interlude from 1979-1983, the Federal Reserve System in the U.S. has targeted interest rates for several decades. While the analysis that follows applies to interest rate targeting more generally, the issue is framed within the context of U.S. monetary policy.

Federal Reserve interest rate targeting conforms to the transmission mechanism described as Model I in the previous chapter. The instrument variable is open market operations (OMO). The operating target is the short-term interest rate (i_{st}). The rate selected for this purpose is the federal funds rate, or the rate on immediately available funds. While it is a nominal interest rate, the intermediate target is the long-term *real* interest rate (r_{lt}). The ultimate policy objectives are the price level and aggregate spending.

The Fed encounters two very difficult problems when attempting to implement policy through this transmission mechanism. First, it is using a nominal interest rate target in a world where rational economic agents think in real terms. The interest rate of importance, then, is the unobservable real interest rate. Second, the transmission of monetary policy occurs across the term structure of interest rates. The operating target is a short-term interest rate, but the critical variable is the long-term rate of interest.

A. The Nominal/Real Dichotomy

The success of Federal Reserve monetary policy is contingent upon control of the real interest rate. Rational economic agents on both sides of the credit market think in real terms and, if one is to change their behavior through policy, it is the real interest rate that counts. Unlike the nominal interest rate, however, the real interest rate is unobservable. The difficulty presented here is that one cannot readily control something that does not lend itself to measurement. That problem is compounded when precision is required. That is generally the case, however, because policymakers employing nominal operating targets most often change those interest rate targets in increments of one-quarter to one-half percent.

Control of the unobservable real rate of interest is hypothesized to occur via changes in the Federal Reserve's nominal interest rate target (the federal funds rate). As noted in Chapter 2, however, the nominal rate of interest, too, is comprised of non-observable components: inflationary expectations; default, money, and income risk premiums; and, time preferences. Each of these components reflects the subjective valuations of millions of market participants. Because subjective valuations of individual economic agents are prone to change, one must operate on the premise that they do. That is, inflationary expectations, risk premiums, and time preferences are incessantly changing.

If these non-observable components of the nominal rate of interest are unstable, when the Fed changes its nominal interest rate target, it cannot know whether the real interest rate is increasing, falling, or staying the same. If a policy-induced higher real interest rate indicates a tighter monetary policy, and a policy-induced lower real rate the opposite, the Federal Reserve does not know whether monetary policy is tighter, easier, or unchanged.

To illustrate, three different scenarios are presented in TABLE 7.1. They are designated as Cases I, II, and III. The first scenario (Case I) is the initial condition. The nominal interest rate is 5 percent, which is also the Fed's targeted interest rate. With a 2 percent expected rate of inflation, the real interest rate is 3 percent. The latter is

TABLE 7.1

The Nominal Interest Rate and Its Components

	i	r	(dp/p)*	risk premium	marginal rate of time preference
Case I	5	3	2	½	2½
Case II	6	4	2	½	3½
Case III	4	2	2	½	1½

apportioned into a risk premium and a marginal rate of time preference.[55]

Assume, initially, that the Federal Reserve tightens monetary policy. In Case II, it raises its target for the nominal interest rate to 6 percent, and provides reserves less liberally to the banking system. With tighter credit conditions, the nominal rate increases to the desired level. Assuming no change in inflationary expectations, the real rate increases to 4 percent. The higher real rate of interest leads to reduced capital goods expenditures, and a higher marginal rate of time preference. In this scenario, the Fed thinks that monetary policy is tighter and, indeed, it is. This is how monetary policy with interest rate targeting is supposed to work.

---

[55] This is the rate of time preference for lenders, which differs from that of borrows in the presence of risk. For a discussion, refer to pp. 49-52.

With the subjective preferences of economic agents constantly changing, however, the world is much more complex than this. For example, do these Case II numbers still constitute tighter monetary policy if the higher real interest rate would have occurred as a result of market activity alone? Commence again with Case I initial conditions, i.e., $i = 5\%$ and $r = 3\%$. Now, assume an increasingly robust economy with businessmen becoming more optimistic. Their increased time preferences for current expenditures are expressed in the form of a greater demand for capital goods. Tighter credit conditions lead to a higher nominal rate (6 percent) and a higher real rate (4 percent). Case II numbers again prevail.

Superimpose upon these events an increase in the Federal Reserve's target for the nominal interest rate---from 5 percent to 6 percent. The Fed's objective is to increase the real interest rate by one percent (from 3 percent to 4 percent). In this case, the Fed does not need to adjust how it is providing reserves to the banking system. The higher interest rates come about through market activity alone, and do not reflect any change in Fed policy. When the Federal Reserve adjusts its interest-rate target upward, that target is simply following the market rate.

This is a case where the Federal Reserve thinks monetary policy is tighter when, in fact, it is not. Errors of this kind are likely when the real interest rate follows a pro cyclical pattern. If business managers and consumers become more optimistic during a business cycle expansion, their greater optimism is expressed in the form of an increase in their time preferences for current expenditures. The real (and nominal) interest rate rises. If the Federal Reserve simultaneously becomes concerned about the exuberant economy, it will move to tighten monetary policy. As in the example above, however, it will erroneously interpret the market-driven rise in interest rates as policy-induced.

The Federal Reserve is prone to making the opposite kind of error when the economy is contracting. Business managers and consumers become more pessimistic. They experience decreases in their time preferences for current expenditures, and the real (and nominal) interest rate falls. The Fed, in an attempt to stimulate aggregate demand, lowers its interest rate target. With the nominal and real rate already falling, the Fed is unable to distinguish market-induced declines in rates from those occasioned by Fed policy.

This scenario is captured in Case III (TABLE 7.1). Commencing with the initial condition (Case I), declines in the real and nominal rate occur in response to reduced time preferences. The nominal rate falls to from 5 to 4 percent; the real rate, from 3 to 2 percent. Simultaneously, the Federal Reserve lowers its target for the nominal interest rate from 5 percent to 4 percent. Its intent is to lower the real rate by a similar amount (from 3 percent to 2 percent). The Federal Reserve does not need to adjust its provision of reserves to the banking system, because both the nominal and real rates reach their targeted levels through market activity. This is a case where the Fed thinks that that monetary policy is easier when, in fact, it is not.

Thus, there are serious reservations concerning the Federal Reserve's ability to effectively control the real rate of interest. When the Fed changes its nominal interest rate target, it does not know with any assurance either the magnitude or direction of policy-induced changes in the real rate of interest.

B. The Term Structure Problem

A second problem the Federal Reserve confronts when targeting interest rates relates to the term structure of interest rates. Not only does the Fed not know whether adjustments in its operating target result in the desired change in the real interest rate, but those policy changes also must be transmitted across the term structure of interest rates. The Federal Reserve's operating target is the short-term nominal rate, but its intermediate target is the *long-term* real interest rate.

The rationale for this transmission mechanism (Model I) is discussed in Chapter 6 above. Outlays for durable goods, both business and consumer, are more easily deferred than are expenditures for non-durable goods. As a consequence, durable goods account for much of the volatility in aggregate spending. Attempts by policy makers to influence aggregate spending (and the price level), then, are geared towards controlling expenditures for those types of goods. With durable goods purchases frequently financed through the issue of long-term bonds, those purchasing durable goods are sensitive to the long-term rate of interest. It follows that, when the Fed employs interest rate targeting, it must target the long-rate.

Precisely how the Federal Reserve successfully navigates the term structure and, simultaneously engineers changes in the real interest rate, is not clear. Moreover, various theories of the term structure (discussed in Chapter 2) do not provide much help. If anything, they cast additional aspersion upon the Fed's ability to successfully implement discretionary policy through interest-rate targeting.

Explanations based on the segmented markets hypothesis, for example, are not encouraging. If market participants adhere strongly to their maturity preferences, there is little likelihood that policy-induced changes in the short-term interest rate target will be transmitted across the term structure to long-term rates of interest. Federal Reserve control, in turn, is marginalized.

On the other hand, information requirements implied under the unbiased expectations and the liquidity preference theories present an even more serious obstacle for those conducting monetary policy. First, the Fed must have prior knowledge of the term structure of inflation premiums and the term structure of risk premiums. Second, it must know how those term structures are changing independent of monetary policy. Finally, it must also know how a given change its short-term interest rate target will affect both of those underlying term structures. Compounding the Fed's information problem is the fact that both inflationary expectations and risk premiums are imbedded in the term structure of interest rates, and not directly observable.

It is clear that the U.S. central bank faces serious information problems when attempting to target long-term real interest rates through use of a short-term nominal operating target. If the Federal Reserve acts as if it can orchestrate desired changes in aggregate spending and the price level through this procedure, it is committing what Friedrich von Hayek called "the pretense of knowledge."[56] It is pretending to know things that, in fact, it does not.

C. A Recent U.S. Case Study

This knowledge problem confronting the Federal Reserve is a good illustration of what happens when the criteria for selecting monetary targets (discussed in the previous

---

[56] Friedrich von Hayek, "The Pretence of Knowledge," *American Economic Review*, 79 (December,1989), 3-7.

chapter) are not satisfied. Because it is not possible to accurately measure the long-term

real interest rate, the Federal Reserve is employing a target it cannot control. Moreover,

lack of knowledge of the long-term real rate also means the linkages in Model I are not

predictable.

U.S. monetary policy from 2004-2006 exemplifies the difficulties encountered

when these monetary target criteria are not met. Starting in June, 2004, the Federal

Reserve increased its target for the federal funds rate fifteen consecutive times. As a

consequence, the federal funds rate target in April, 2006 was 4.75 percent versus 1.00

percent in the first half of 2004. Those changes are chronicled in Table 7.2.

Many observers routinely describe these upward adjustments in the federal funds

rate target as tighter monetary policy. There are serious doubts, however, about such an

interpretation. It is true that other short-term nominal rates increased along with the

federal funds rate. The 3-month Treasury-bill rate, for example, rose from 1.17 percent

to 4.60 percent between June 1, 2004 and March 1, 2006.[57]

But, as previously noted, higher short-term nominal interest rates do not

necessarily mean tighter monetary policy. Long-term nominal interest rates actually fell

during the same 21-month period. The rate for 20-year U.S. Treasury securities declined

from 5.45 percent to 4.74 percent. These changes in both long-term and short-term rates

for U.S. Treasury securities are reflected in FIGURE 7.1. It depicts the shapes of the

term structure of interest rates for U.S. Treasury securities on both June 1, 2004 and

March 1, 2006. The yield curve became noticeably flatter.

---

[57] Interest rates are for constant maturities. Source: Board of Governors of the Federal Reserve System.

TABLE 7.2

Federal Funds Rate Target

Date	Level (percent)
2006	
March 28	4.75
January 31	4.50
2005	
December 13	4.25
November 01	4.00
September 20	3.75
August 09	3.50
June 30	3.25
May 03	3.00
March 22	2.75
February 02	2.50
2004	
December 14	2.25
November 10	2.00
September 21	1.75
August 10	1.50
June 30	1.25
2003	
June 25	1.00

Source: Board of Governors of the Federal Reserve System

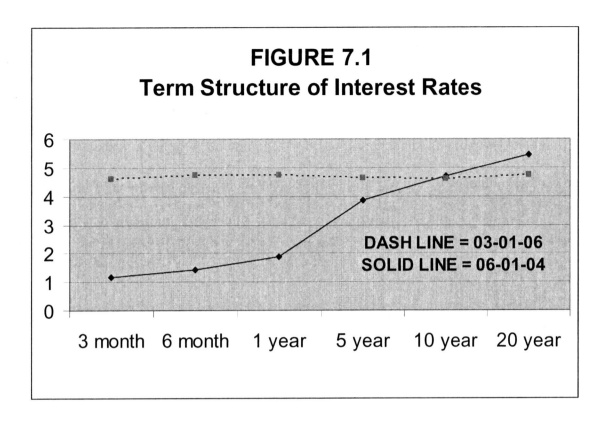

FIGURE 7.1
Term Structure of Interest Rates

DASH LINE = 03-01-06
SOLID LINE = 06-01-04

3 month 6 month 1 year 5 year 10 year 20 year

Lower long-term nominal interest rates, however, are not the issue. It is long-term real interest rates, and not nominal rates, that are critical for economic decision-makers. If monetary policy was, indeed, tighter during this 21-month period, long-term real interest rates must have increased while nominal rates were falling. Moreover, the increase in real rates must have occurred as a result of monetary policy and not due to other factors such as an increase in default risk or changes in time preferences for current expenditure. While such a scenario appears doubtful, no one knows for certain. Hence, the appropriate answer to the question about whether monetary policy is tighter is: "I don't know."

II. Friedman: Rules vs. Discretion

Milton Friedman argues that the adoption of fiat money has led to much economic instability. The problem, though, is not the use of fiat money. Rather, it is the procedures employed by central banks to implement monetary policy, specifically their use of discretionary policies. Replacing discretionary monetary policy with a monetary rule would greatly reduce economic uncertainty, especially concerning future monetary policy. This would provide a much better climate for productive activity and eliminate much of the economic instability occasioned by the use of fiat money.

In fashioning his position, Friedman's posture is diametrically opposed to those who favor the use of discretionary policy. Proponents of discretionary policy maintain that its use can greatly improve macroeconomic performance. Appropriate application of policy instruments will both reduce short-run business cycle fluctuations and bring us greater long-run price stability. Monetary stimulation during a recession, for example, will shorten the recession. If too much inflation is the problem, tighter monetary policy is in order.

Friedman's case against discretionary policy is that those implementing such policies most often do the wrong thing. Two principal reasons for this are: 1) politics, and 2) ignorance. By doing the wrong thing, those implementing discretionary policies make economic conditions worse rather than better.

A. Politics

Economic analysis of monetary policy often proceeds as if this policy were conducted in a political vacuum. That decidedly is not the case. Monetary policy is carried out by government, and the political consequences of a policy action receive careful consideration. What is considered rational policy from a political perspective can differ significantly from that implied by economic theory. If political considerations dominate, those implementing discretionary policy may, with good reason, deliberately select the incorrect economic policy.

Political considerations can affect monetary policy even in countries (such as the United States) that have a fairly independent central bank. When, for example, is a good time for the central bank to invoke a tighter monetary policy that results in higher nominal interest rates? From a political perspective, the likely answer is never. As a consequence, central bankers bold enough to undertake such policies can expect politicians to sharply criticize their actions. That may be enough for policy-makers contemplating such action to reconsider.

Elections cycles also create problems for those conducting discretionary monetary policy. In the absence of political pressure, introducing a policy change too close to an election can be interpreted as politically motivated. For central bankers in democratic countries who are sensitive to such charges, this might inhibit the implementation of an otherwise appropriate change in monetary policy.

A second way that election cycles influence monetary policy is through the actions of politicians concerned about an imminent election. They might exert pressure on central bankers to undertake policies favorable to their election (or reelection). Research conducted by Robert Weintraub suggests that this may be the rule rather than the exception in the U.S. For the period from 1951 to the end of the 1970s, he found that changes in Presidential administrations generally resulted in changes in monetary policy in a direction consistent with the economic views of the President.[58] Given that Ronald Regan ran on a platform of reducing inflation, Paul Volker's disinflationary policies in the 1980s are an indication that Weintraub's results extend beyond his sample period.

A prototypical case study in central bank accommodation was President Richard Nixon's reelection campaign in 1972. Inflation was increasing at the time, and economic theory implied a tighter monetary policy. Tighter money, however, was not the policy of choice for President Nixon. From his perspective, such policies had cost him the Presidential election in 1960. He was not interested in a repeat of that experience. Federal Reserve Chairman Arthur Burns accommodated President Nixon's desire that monetary policy not be tightened. Nixon won the election, but at a considerable cost to the economy.

B. Ignorance

A second reason for the failure of discretionary policies is ignorance. The existence of time lags presents a major problem for those attempting to implement discretionary policies. These lags imply that policy carried out today has its impact in the future. Selection of the appropriate policy, then, requires the ability to forecast accurately. Economists, however, are notoriously weak when it comes to forecasting

---

[58] Weintraub, R. E., "Congressional Supervision of Monetary Policy," *Journal of Monetary Economics*, 4 (April, 1978), 341-362.

future economic activity. This ignorance is especially pronounced for turning points in the economy, where one would anticipate significant changes in discretionary policy.

Three time lags encountered when implementing discretionary policy are the recognition lag, the execution lag, and the impact lag. To illustrate the difficulties introduced by these time lags, refer to FIGURE 7.2. Real GDP (y) is plotted against time (t). The business cycle peak occurs at time t_1, with GDP equal to y_1.

The decline in economic activity commencing at time t_1 is not discovered until time t_2. One reason for this lag is that published economic data generally are a record of

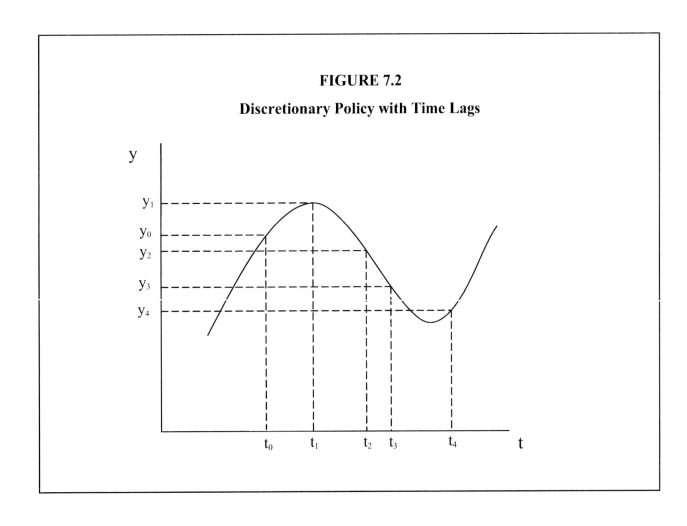

FIGURE 7.2

Discretionary Policy with Time Lags

253

the past, and turning points in economic activity often are not discovered in these data until well after they happen. For this cycle, the time interval $(t_2 - t_1)$ is the recognition lag. It is the time that elapses between when the economy changes, and when policy makers know about the change.

The policy response is not instantaneous. In the case of monetary policy, the central bank must both adopt a new policy and implement that policy. These events, too, require time. Assume that the policy response, which is additional monetary stimulation, occurs at time t_3. The time interval $(t_3 - t_2)$, then, is the execution lag. This is the amount time that elapses between recognition of the problem and when policy makers undertake appropriate policy action.

The impact of this policy action, likewise, is not instantaneous. Rather than occurring at a point in time, it is distributed over a period of time. The precise timing of the impact is unknown. Friedman's estimates for the U.S. economy are that it will have little (or no) impact for the first 9-12 months, with the total impact occurring over a period of years.

Simplifying, assume that the impact of monetary policy does occur at a single point in time (t_4). By that time, the economy has already entered the expansionary phase of the business cycle. To moderate business cycle fluctuations, this phase of the cycle calls for monetary restraint. Instead of monetary restraint, however, the central bank is providing monetary stimulus. It has done the wrong thing. Monetary policy will accentuate the business cycle upswing and, in doing so, it increases the amplitude of the business cycle.

Given the existence of these time lags, appropriate discretionary policy for this economic cycle requires that the central bank undertake simulative policy before the business cycle downturn occurs, e.g., at time t_0. The wisdom to do so, however, requires that (central bank) economists correctly forecast the impending peak at t_1. Their inability to accurately forecast turning points, or ignorance, generally precludes that.

C. Friedman's x-Percent Money Growth Rule

Even though it is inadvertent, central bank implementation of discretionary monetary policy often makes things worse rather than better. For that reason, Friedman recommends scrapping discretionary policy. In its place, the central bank should follow a rule and increase the money supply at a constant rate. If, for example, a rate of 4 percent is selected, the central bank increases the money supply 4 percent each year. That is Friedman's x-percent money growth rule.

The particular growth rate that is selected is less important than selecting one. A rate in the neighborhood of 4 percent may be desirable, however, because it approximates the secular growth rate for production. Synchronizing the growth of money and output would permit (proximate) long-run price stability.

Friedman maintains that the potential benefits of employing a monetary growth rule are enormous. The principal one is a more stable economy. A volatile monetary policy contributes to economic instability, thus increasing the amplitude of the business cycle. Use of a monetary rule effectively eliminates this source of cyclical instability.

A second benefit is increased long-run economic growth. As monetary policy becomes more predictable, the uncertainty faced by those in private business is greatly diminished. This lowers the risk premium in interest rates, and will increase the rate of capital formation in the economy. More capital formation leads to increased worker productivity and higher living standards.

Finally, use of a monetary rule will eliminate of secular inflation. Had the Federal Reserve employed such a rule in the past half-century, the great depreciation that occurred in the purchasing power of the U.S. dollar would have been avoided. Elimination of secular inflation will enhance the services provided by money, especially those eroded by unremitting inflation.

Despite these potential benefits, Friedman is aware of the forces militating against adoption of a monetary rule. A major force is the spiritual legacy of the Enlightenment. The great scientific and economic achievements of the past several centuries have nurtured the sense that man has the ability to make things better through manipulation and control. When placed in a monetary context, this perspective makes it easier for central bankers to inspire confidence in their ability to successfully manage monetary affairs.

Public confidence in central bank stewardship is reinforced by central bank resistance to a monetary rule. Given the complexities of a modern economy, central bankers are often given much greater credit for their ability to manipulate the aggregate economic activity than is warranted by experience. The general public often basks in the comfort of a central bank that is "in control." As human beings, it is natural that central bankers find such deference to their skills and influence quite flattering. It is contrary to human nature to expect them to embrace the prospect of replacing their reasoned judgments with a mechanical procedure that greatly diminishes their social significance.

III. Rational Expectations

Economists know that a person's expectations affect the economic decisions made by that individual. Rational expectations theory is concerned with how those expectations are formed and, also, how economists model those expectations. Much of this theory was developed in response to the use of large macroeconometric models (by business and government). Statistical in form, these models were an adjunct to the Keynesian revolution in macroeconomic theory. The models often contained several hundred equations, and were used for forecasting purposes. Keynesian economists used the models to advise governments about the consequences of different activist policies, while those in the private sector used them as an aid in business decision-making.

Many of the equations in macroeconometric models were behavioral in nature. That necessitated the modeling of expectations, even though those expectations were largely unknown. Proxies for these unknown expectations were most often obtained by assuming that economic agents have adaptive expectations. With this approach, the expected value of a variable was estimated as a weighted sum of past values of that same variable. Historical time series data were employed for rendering concrete estimates.

Econometric models constructed using this methodology often result in large forecasting errors, and economists in the rational expectations tradition have a ready explanation for this. Reliance on adaptive expectations as a proxy for actual expectations is an inherent weakness of the models. For, modeling human behavior in this way is tantamount to assuming that economic agents are irrational. The reason is that economic agents with adaptive expectations make systematic errors. That is, they repeatedly make the same mistakes.

An alternative to assuming that expectations are adaptive is to assume they are rational. Rational individuals are not restricted to using past information (such as past values of variables) when forming their expectations. Their expectations are formed by taking into account all information that is worthwhile acquiring. Agents behaving in this fashion are said to have rational expectations. Once the models of economists incorporate rational expectations, economic agents no longer make systematic errors. Moreover, such rational behavior has important implications for the conduct of economic policy.

If economic policy affects economic agents in a significant way, then it is rational for them to take the effects of that policy into account. Furthermore, if those administering policy behave consistently, economic agents will learn how that policy is implemented under different economic circumstances. Once they do, individuals will adjust their behavior to the policy, and make necessary behavioral changes *before* any change in policy is undertaken. Because adjustment to the policy has already taken place, no behavioral response follows any predictable change in economic policy. In rational expectations theory, this result is known as the Policy Impotence Theorem.

Where behavior is rational in this sense, discretionary policy loses its effectiveness. In the case of U.S. monetary policy, economic agents (such as portfolio managers) adjust to Federal Reserve actions before those actions occur. The resultant is that changes in Fed policy have no (subsequent) impact on real aggregate spending. With discretionary monetary having no "teeth," rational expectations theorists often accept Friedman's concept of a monetary rule as the preferred course of action.

This argument against the use of discretionary policy is somewhat different than that of Milton Friedman (and the monetarists). In Friedman's case, policy does not work because policymakers are either ignorant or subject to political influence. For the rational expectations economists, it is because those affected by economic policy are so smart (or rational).

IV. The Austrian Perspective

Economists in the Austrian tradition generally favor "hard money." They find it vexing that a monetary economist such as Milton Friedman favors reliance upon markets everywhere except in his area of expertise, the realm of money. The Austrian position is that money is too important to be left to government. Instead, money and all monetary relations should be determined through exchange activities in the marketplace. Because fiduciary money was a spontaneous market development, and fiat money was not, Austrians generally favor reestablishing fiduciary money by returning to the gold standard.

If the quantity of money and all monetary relations are determined by market participants, government has no monetary role. There is no monetary policy. For that reason, Austrians are against all monetary policy as practiced under fiat money regimes. That would include Friedman's monetary rule as well as all variations of discretionary policy.

At the center of the Austrian critique of monetary policy is the concept of the price level. The importance attached to the idea of an average price dates back to the early twentieth century, when Irving Fisher argued that the value of money should be standardized.[59] By this, he meant that the objective of government monetary policy should be to stabilize the average price, or the price level. While Fisher was unsuccessful in his crusade to standardize money, the concept of the price level subsequently assumed a life of its own. After governments mandated the use of fiat money, the price level became a variable subject to manipulation by monetary authorities.

Despite the efforts by central banks to manage the price level, Austrians give the concept little credence. For them, the price level has no significance independent of its component parts---the individual prices. To the extent that there is an average price, it is an aggregation of these individual prices. In a market setting, each individual price has meaning, or informational content. Each is an expression of the subjective valuation that individuals have placed on that object. Viewed collectively, a set of individual prices represents relative valuations.

With no rigid dichotomy separating micro and macroeconomics, the significance Austrians attach to individual prices is not restricted to the realm of microeconomics. They are equally important in a macroeconomic setting. Hence, when central banks manipulate the price level, without regard to its constituent parts, they destroy the informational content of individual prices. In doing so, they disrupt the critical role that prices play in coordinating the diverse economic activities that collectively make up the aggregate economy.

---

[59] In the spirit of the enlightenment, Fisher maintained that "our unstable and unstandardized monetary units are among the last remnants of barbarism and are out of place in present-day civilization." Fisher, Irving, "Stabilizing the Dollar," *American Economic Review*, 9 (March, 1919), 156-157.

Assume, for example, that a central bank employs monetary policy to stabilize the average price. The problem here is that market participants may have preferences that are not consistent with an unchanged exchange value for money. In the absence of monetary policy, they may have valued money either more highly or less highly than before. If they valued money more highly, their preferences were consistent with deflation rather than price stability. Alternatively, placing a lower value on money would result in inflation.

When money is a strictly a market phenomenon, inflation, deflation, and price stability are all possible outcomes. Moreover, there is no analytical basis for favoring one of these outcomes over the others. This view is antithetical to conventional thinking, especially with regard to deflation. Most contemporary policymakers, and many economists, consider deflation highly undesirable---something that must be avoided at all costs.

The source of this bias against deflation is the Great Depression experience, when deflation was accompanied by an unprecedented drop in production. To generalize from this episode, however, is ahistorical. Data generally do not affirm such a linkage between deflation and economic decline.[60] Moreover, given our experiences with fiat money, it seems much more likely that massive economic decline would be accompanied by hyperinflation rather than deflation.

As a consequence, Austrians do not readily dismiss deflation when it is the natural outcome of economic activity. Deflation generally occurs when a country's growth rate for production exceeds the growth rate of money. Money becomes more scarce in

---

[60] See Andrew Atkeson and Patrick J. Kehoe, "Deflation and Depression: Is There an Empirical Link?," *American Economic Review: Papers and Proceedings*, 94 (May, 2004), 99-103. Using data for 17 countries and covering more than 100 years, they find virtually no link between deflation and depression.

relation to goods, and that tends to occasion an increase money's exchange value. This happened in the U.S. during the last third of the nineteenth century. The country was on the gold standard, and there were few new discoveries of gold to augment the world's gold supply.

Data for this period, assembled by Christina D. Romer, appear in TABLE 7.3. Deflation averaged 1.36 percent per year from 1869 to 1899. In contrast to the conventional view of deflation, this period of falling prices was not one of economic

TABLE 7.3

Prices and Production in the U.S.: 1869-1899
(percent change)

Years	Real GNP	GNP-Implicit Price Deflator
1869-1879	5.38	- 3.23
1879-1889	3.21	0.03
1889-1899	3.82	- 0.85
1869-1899	4.13	- 1.36

Source: Christina D. Romer, "The Prewar Cycle Reconsidered: New Estimates of Gross National Product: 1869-1908," *Journal of Political Economy*, pp. 1-37, February, 1989.

calamity, or even malaise. Instead, it was a period characterized by much innovation and very rapid industrialization. The average growth rate for production was considerably higher than average growth during the twentieth century. Moreover, production growth was, by far, most rapid in the decade with the highest rate of deflation (1869-1879).

Historical episodes like this suggest that changes in the general price level (such as inflation or deflation) generally do not cause problems when they are driven by market forces. A collateral issue, though, is whether problems arise when the source of the price-level change is monetary manipulation by the central bank, and not market adjustments occurring in response to changing market conditions.

Austrians answer this question in the affirmative. Consider, initially, what happens when changes in the quantity of money are a derivative of the market process. Allocation of additional esources to the production of new money, in this case, originates with decisions made by individual market participants. As a response to market demand, the additional money was, in a sense, "ordered" by those market participants. It reflects their preferences concerning the use of scarce resources. Any change in prices brought about by the new money is, likewise, a part of the same market process whereby individual plans and preferences are rendered consistent with one another.

The situation is entirely different when the source of a change in money is the central bank. In this case, the additional money is not ordered by market participants. As a consequence, it is not a part of the market adjustment process that renders individual plans consistent with one another. Instead, the new money is a disruptive force in markets. By changing prices, relative to what they otherwise would have been, it destroys the informational content of market prices. Relative prices no longer represent that delicate balance necessary to coordinate economic activity across markets.

A critical price often distorted by monetary policy is the real interest rate. This rate reflects the time preferences of market participants. A given real rate specifies how much future consumption economic agents are willing to sacrifice in order to have more present consumption. By affecting how consumers distribute consumption across time, the real interest rate plays an essential role in the intertemporal allocation of resources.

When monetary policy brings about a change in the real interest rate, it adversely affects the intertemporal allocation of resources. It does so by distorting the informational content present in a market-determined real rate of interest rate. The new real interest rate occasioned by monetary policy emits the "wrong" signal to market participants, and the economic coordination brought about by market prices is disrupted. Production plans of firms are no longer consistent with the preferences of their customers.

The disruptive influence of monetary policy is illustrated by comparing situations with and without monetary policy. The market under scrutiny is the loanable funds market. Prior to the introduction of monetary policy, the real interest rate plays its allocative role. In doing so, it renders the plans of all economic agents consistent with one another. Those plans are reflected in the demand and supply curves D and S in FIGURE 7.3.

Plan consistency occurs at the market clearing rate r_0. The quantity of loanable funds supplied, S_0, shows abstinence from present consumption by economic agents. It is exactly equal to the quantity of loanable funds demanded, D_0. This demand originates

FIGURE 7.3

Market for Loanable Funds

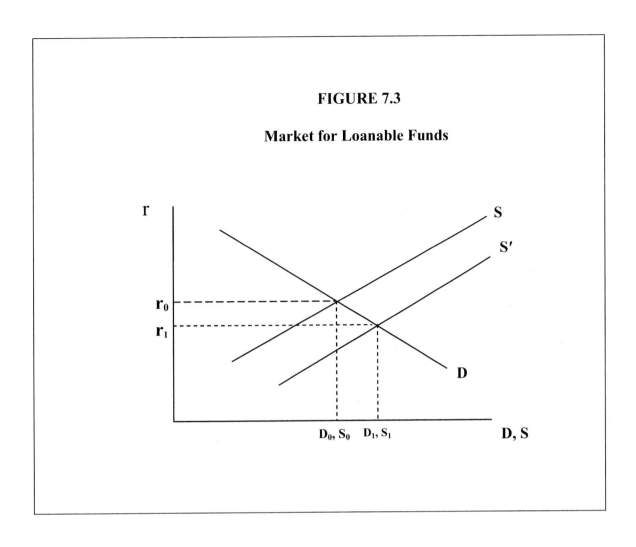

with consumers desirous of consuming more than their incomes, and producers borrowing to acquire capital goods.

Intertemporal economic coordination occurs in this case because the real interest rate is transmitting the correct information to market participants. The amount of resources released from (net) present consumption is precisely absorbed by those borrowing to purchase capital goods. Those abstaining from present consumption are choosing an increased amount of future consumption. That demand for future consumer goods will be accommodated by a larger volume of future output made possible by current capital formation.

Such intertemporal coordination of economic activity no longer prevails once monetary policy is introduced. The reason is that the information contained in the real interest rate is distorted by monetary policy. To show this, assume the central bank increases the money supply. The supply curve for loanable funds shifts to the right (to S'). There is now an excess supply of loanable funds at r_0, and the real interest rate falls to r_1.

While this lower real interest rate does clear the credit market, the rate did not fall due to any change in the plans of individual economic agents. It did not fall, for example, because consumers desire to defer more consumption to the future, or because producers choose to purchase fewer capital goods. A lower real interest in either of those circumstances would convey such a change in preferences to others in the market.

Instead, the source of the decline in the real interest rate is the additional funds made available through monetary policy. By falling without any changes in the plans of economic agents, the informational content of the real interest rate is compromised. At r_1, the real interest rate is below the level (r_0) that renders the diverse plans of economic agents consistent with one another. The new real interest rate is transmitting the "wrong" signals to market participants.

Producers are encouraged to purchase more capital goods, and they bid the necessary resources away from those producing consumer goods. The problem is that this redirection of resources is not consistent with consumer preferences. Consumers have not chosen to tradeoff additional present consumption for more future consumption.

This miscommunication brought about by monetary policy has important macroeconomic consequences. At some point, this misallocation of resources will have to be rectified. The endplay involves economic recession with all of its attributes---falling (and possibly negative) profits, idle capital goods, unemployment, and business bankruptcies.

From the Austrian perspective, then, all monetary policy is disruptive rather than beneficial. By impacting relative prices, it destroys the informational content of those prices. This has unsalutary macroeconomic consequences. Resources are misallocated in the sense that what is produced in the economy is inconsistent with the preferences of those purchasing that output.

Unfortunately, to undo the pernicious effects of such monetary policy (or to reallocate those resources) is not a costless proposition. Requisite adjustments in the allocation of resources are similar to those that occur at the end of a protracted war. Large quantities of resources are misallocated in the sense that they are used to produce war materials that are no longer useful. These situations often lead to a period of falling output and increased unemployment.

V. Postscript

These critiques raise serious doubts about the efficacy of monetary policy. The limitations faced by monetary authorities, as enumerated in these critiques, are not generally reflected in the sentiments of the general public. In the U.S., for example, Federal Reserve officials are generally held in high esteem, and there is limited skepticism regarding the credibility of Federal Reserve policy. The public seems contented with their belief that the Fed is "in control."

That faith in the control exercised by monetary authorities is warranted only if the critiques presented here generally are erroneous. From analytical perspective, however, those critiques are not so easily dismissed. Consequently, there remains a significant disconnect between views frequently held by the public and those expounded by critics of monetary policy.

To illustrate, consider an example that captures the views of the general public. The economy is sluggish and the Federal Reserve decides to stimulate aggregate spending. The transmission mechanism employed by the Fed is Model I, the "Keynesian" transmission mechanism (Chapter 6). Linkages involve open market operations, the short-term interest rate (the federal funds rate), the long-term interest rate, and aggregate spending on durable goods.

To stimulate aggregate demand, the Federal Reserve supplies more reserves to the banking system by purchasing Treasury securities in the open market. The increased availability of bank reserves leads to an excess supply of funds in the federal funds market, causing banks lend to one another at a lower federal funds rate. This lower nominal rate works itself across the maturity spectrum, and the long-term real interest rate declines. Business and consumers respond to this incentive and purchase more durable goods. Real aggregate spending rises.

In this scenario, monetary policy works. The Fed clearly is in control, and the public's confidence in the Federal Reserve policy is vindicated. If this is how monetary policy generally works, problems with targeting real interest rates and the admonitions of

Friedman, rational expectations theorists, and the Austrians concerning the limitations of monetary policy are irrelevant. Rejection of those critiques implies the following:

- The unobservable long-term real interest rate is amenable to control by the Federal Reserve.

- Monetary policy is driven by economic considerations, and is generally unaffected by politics.

- While individuals in the private sector are unable to accurately forecast the future (and especially business cycle turning points), individuals employed by the Federal Reserve can.

- Even though economic agents in the private sector are affected in a dramatic way by monetary policy, they make no attempt to anticipate and respond to future Federal Reserve policy.

- The role that prices, such as the interest rate, play in the coordination of economic activity can be safely disregarded by monetary authorities.

From a market-oriented perspective, these propositions make little sense. It, likewise, makes little sense to accept the much more tentative view that the conduct of monetary policy is not really science, but more like an art. That analogy is weak because artists exercise considerable control over the work they fashion. It is a degree of control that greatly exceeds what monetary authorities possess. To suggest, on the other hand, that those conducting monetary policy are "shooting in the dark" is, perhaps, an overstatement, too. But, it is probably a good deal closer to reality than considering their work some kind of artistic endeavor.